Best Pub Walks in Lancashire

Neil Coates

Published by Sigma Leisure – an imprint of
Sigma Press, 1 South Oak Lane, Wilmslow, Cheshire SK9 6AR, England.

British Library Cataloguing in Publication Data
A CIP record for this book is available from the British Library.

ISBN: 1-85058-799-X

Typesetting and Design by: Sigma Press, Wilmslow, Cheshire.

Cover photograph: The Black Dog at Belmont – a popular destination for ramblers in the West Pennines *(Photograph: Clive Weake).* The Red Rose is the emblem of Lancashire and is reproduced with permission from the Friends of Real Lancashire.

Maps and photographs: Neil Coates

Printed by: MFP Design and Print

Disclaimer: the information in this book is given in good faith and is believed to be correct at the time of publication. No responsibility is accepted by either the author or publisher for errors or omissions, or for any loss or injury howsoever caused. Only you can judge your own fitness, competence and experience. Do not rely solely on sketch maps for navigation: we strongly recommend the use of appropriate Ordnance Survey (or equivalent) maps.

Foreword

How does one define Lancashire? Some will mistakenly think of that limited area of the country currently administered by Lancashire County Council, which excludes large areas of the traditional county, but does include parts of Yorkshire. More enlightened folk will consider the Real County, which still stretches from the River Mersey in the south to the River Duddon and the centre of Windermere in the north.

This confusion about the true identity of Lancashire and other traditional counties dates back to 1974 when dramatic changes to local government areas took place. However, these and subsequent changes did not alter the boundaries of traditional counties, as confirmed by the following official statement:

"The Local Government Act 1972 did not abolish traditional counties, only administrative ones. Although for local government purposes some of the historic counties have ceased to be administrative areas, they continue to exist for other purposes." – *Department of the Environment 3.9.1991*

Unfortunately, the Ordnance Survey changed its mapping policy after 1974 and chose to depict administrative areas on maps, instead of the traditional counties as it had previously done. This led people to think that Lancashire had shrunk overnight, with large areas of the county being labelled as somewhere else! More recently, in 1998, the new unitary authorities of Blackpool and Blackburn with Darwen were created and left administrative Lancashire, with the consequence that their areas are no longer mapped as a part of the county. What a farce this policy is, and what confusion it has created.

The Friends of Real Lancashire actively promote the true identity of the traditional county of Lancashire, whose boundaries are the same as the County Palatine of Lancaster. Many official statements have been issued, confirming that the boundaries of the traditional county and the County Palatine remain unaltered. So be assured that wherever you live, drink or walk within the traditional county boundaries, you are still in Real Lancashire. As the author acknowledges, whilst some of the locations in this book are labelled for administrative purposes as being in Lancashire, they are in fact in Yorkshire.

For more information contact The Friends of Real Lancashire, 1 Belvidere Park, Great Crosby, Lancashire, L23 0SP. E-mail: csd@forl.co.uk – or visit our website: www.forl.co.uk

Chris Dawson – Chairman, The Friends of Real Lancashire

Preface

Lancashire is both a geographical area and a state of mind. Those born in the Red Rose County are fiercely proud of the fact and generally choose to dissociate themselves from the foibles of latter-day local government eccentricities. After all, England's greatest cricketing side is still based at Old Trafford – could this be anything but in Lancashire? And the greatest football teams – can they logically be saddled with addresses in Greater Manchester or Merseyside? To all those of sound mind, Lancashire still stretches from the Mersey to the high peaks of the Lake District

This pride also extends to the countryside. Yet the county is only now coming into its own and being discovered, by both residents and visitors alike, as the very best of countryside walking areas. Geographically, the county is one of the most diverse in Britain: from the eerie windswept marshes of the coast to the high moors of the Pennines, the craggy limestone country in the north to the lush, sinuous valleys of the Hodder, Ribble and Lune there's countryside for virtually all tastes. Even local ramblers are constantly amazed at new discoveries around every corner.

"Best Pub Walks in Lancashire" aims to share aspects of all these landscapes with you, with the additional bonanza of a few hours whiled away in convivial country hostelries. The walks themselves are not claimed to be necessarily the most scenic or challenging in the county, nor the pubs necessarily the best; obviously such things are purely subjective. I've sought to combine walks and pubs which should give you an excellent taste of that which Lancashire has to offer in terms of walking and of good beer; with some the pub was the prime mover and a walk fitted in around, with others the walk was the target. A good geographical spread was the aim, but I make no apologies for excluding town pubs and walks or some very well known countryside spots in the Lake District – this area is covered in the Sigma Leisure companion volumes "Best Pub Walks in the Lakeland Fringes" and "Best Pub Walks in The Lake District".

Most of the walks are readily accessible on a regular basis by public transport from one or more of the main towns in Lancashire;

where possible I've indicated in the titles of each walk the relevant rail service to use. For specific train times call the national enquiry line 08457 484950. Bus services are generally too prone to changes to make detailing them here worthwhile. Your best bet is to ring the local enquiry number for the area (in the phone book) or the national enquiry line (0870 608 2608) for up-to-date information. If you're travelling by car then almost all the pubs featured have a dedicated car park where you can park up whilst you enjoy the walk, provided, of course, that you intend to use the pub before you set out or when you return breathless and thirsty; if you get the chance, have a word with the landlord before you set out. At the few which do not have a car park, there is safe roadside parking or a village car park nearby.

Most of the research for this book was undertaken during the winter, an unbeatable time to walk when the sun is up and the ground crisp with frost or snow – but it can be atrociously muddy. My heartfelt thanks go to the landladies and landlords whose irrepressible forbearance at the sight of the author and companions tramping yet another field full of mud into their floor (despite valiant attempts to clean boots at the door) was matched by their knowledge of the pub's history, the local area and by their innkeeping skills.

Thanks also to my walking companions and route-testers, Bev Ridyard, Paul Richardson and Fred Laugharne, whose diligence in sampling bar meals and real ales proved formidable; to Clive Weake and Nick Osborne at the County Countryside Unit. Finally, a particular expression of gratitude to Jenny and Terry Reilly for hospitality above and beyond the call of duty on numerous visits during the course of research.

Neil Coates

Contents

Introduction

The Walks

Introduction

Whither Lancashire?

As an entity, Lancashire goes back only to the 12th century when the lands between the Mersey and Duddon rivers were first treated as one for exchequer purposes and essentially controlled by one individual, John, Count of Mortain, later King John. The history of the area is, of course, infinitely older. Stone circles, cairns, hill forts and tumuli testify to pre-historic settlement; the Romans left a legacy of forts and roads; Scandinavian place names from the 8th to 11th centuries abound and there are records, albeit meagre, in the Domesday survey of 1086 (for the purposes of which lands south of the Ribble were counted as Cheshire and north of the Ribble as Yorkshire, perish the thought). A century after King John another John, the redoubtable John of Gaunt, established the county as a Palatinate, virtually a self-governing state within England with its own judicial system. Such powers continued for centuries afterwards in the guise of the Duchy of Lancaster; problems caused by this contributed to the Wars of the Roses in the 15th century.

From the 15th to the 17th centuries Lancashire, in most respects, mirrored the development of much of the rest of England. The population grew steadily, if slowly, estimates suggest around 200,000 in 1690 of which perhaps one in six lived in towns. In the countryside, a rich and diverse agricultural base developed which has left a strong legacy to this day. Catholicism remained the dominant religious trait, but with a strong Puritan element developing in the towns; this divide was reflected in the Civil War, which proved largely town against country in the region. In one area, however, Lancashire differed from most of the rest of England. Few guilds or corporations gained precedence in the towns or countryside meaning that the county was essentially a free trade area where anyone could trade in anything without the necessity to make recourse to guild membership or training. This was to have a profound effect on the county.

The 18th and 19th centuries saw the county rise to prominence, thanks to the textile industries. The foundations of such were laid in those non-guild days of the previous two centuries with the unfettered development of the linen industry on the coastal plain, the woollen industry in the rural West Pennine area and the fustian (a mixture of cotton with linen or wool) industry to the north of Manchester. It was this latter manufacture that led to the growth of the cotton industry – King Cotton – for which the county became world-renowned. The inventive minds of Arkwright, Kay and Crompton nurtured the birth of the Industrial Revolution in Lancashire which was to sweep England to World dominance under Victoria, a dominance powered and funded largely by the north west. The period also saw the rapid development of the "Cotton Towns" and the growth of Manchester and Liverpool as major world cities. Other important industries developed in tandem with textiles – coal mining, heavy engineering, steelmaking and shipbuilding – but all are now largely poignant memories; the county has suffered more than most from the economic changes, traits and absurdities of past decades.

Politics dealt Lancashire a severe blow in 1974 when the administrative county was dismembered following the Maud Commission report. At a stroke, the county appeared to lose Manchester and Liverpool, many of the cotton towns and a large chunk of southern Lakeland. The county boundary that runs up the middle of Windermere also seemed to be lost, together with Coniston Water – the county's largest lake. You will find few supporters of this local government gerrymandering today: Mancunians and Liverpudlians alike remain staunchly Lancastrian, as do people in southern Lakeland. Conversely, the same changes saw administrative Lancashire landed with parts of Yorkshire; large areas of Bowland appeared to change from White to Red Rose overnight, and a similar plight befell residents of Saddleworth, east of Oldham. Many of the good burghers in the communities north of Clitheroe still claim to be Yorkshire born and bred and, uniquely, males born after 1974 in the Saddleworth area (now in Greater Manchester) can still play cricket for Yorkshire as home-born sons. Some of the walks in this book dip into these extraneous areas.

This historical complexity is matched by the county's landscapes. Its highest points at over 2000ft rank as mountains, whilst parts of the south-west are below sea level. The sharp, sudden contrasts between coastal lowlands and moorland blocs are unmatched anywhere whilst some of the secluded and sheltered upland valleys generate their own microclimates. Two of England's great rivers, the Lune and the Ribble, drain vast tracts of countryside little changed by the hand of man; relatively few roads cross or follow these waterways resulting in a legacy of unspoilt landscapes. The coastline hosts some of Britain's most spectacular sand dunes, greatest salt marshes, and sand flats; it lacks only high cliffs but the coastal limestone crags of the north-west are equally evocative.

The Breweries

In common with every other county, Lancashire has seen its share of traditional local and regional breweries devastated since the second war. Such decline has seen the demise of local favourites like Bents, Duttons, Almonds, Magees, Matthew Brown, Yates & Jackson and Mitchells. The only survivor of this carnage is Thwaites of Blackburn, still brewing at The Star Brewery nearly 200 years after its foundation.

Even famous regional brewers such as Chesters, Wilsons, Higsons and Oldham have succumbed to the rule of faceless accountants and profiteers. True, products bearing some of these names are still available in Lancashire but they are simply names used by the marketeers of the major multinational breweries who took them over, asset-stripped them and then closed them down. Higsons, that most Liverpudlian of beers, is now brewed in Warrington; Wilsons' Manchester Ale in Mansfield, all at the expense of taste, price and choice for the consumer. Nor has this trend subsided. In the past decade nationally known names such as Greenall Whitley and Boddingtons have sold their brewing interests to concentrate on pub and leisure management; Greenalls is now brewed by Carlsberg-Tetley, Boddingtons by Whitbread. Thankfully some regional brewers seek to remain locally based and continue to serve the interests of their local drinkers – Thwaites in the centre of the county and Burtonwood (brewed in north Cheshire) in the south. Cains took over the former Higsons brewery in Liverpool and has a dedicated following in south Lancashire (and elsewhere!).

Fortunately, Lancashire is well blessed with free houses and the products of well over 100 brewery companies – about a quarter of all the breweries in the country – can be sampled somewhere in the county. Thus favourites nationally such as Marston's, Theakston's and Sam Smith's can be sampled alongside more parochial beers from the likes of Joseph Holt, Hyde's and Lees (all long-established family breweries in old Lancashire, now Greater Manchester), Phoenix and Moorhouse's.

These latter two breweries are in the vanguard of what has proved to be a thriving resurgence of the ancient and noble tradition of small-scale brewing in Lancashire. There is anything up to a dozen pub-based or industrial-unit based breweries in the county. Phoenix (actually just in Greater Manchester at Heywood) and Moorhouses (Burnley) brew a great range of beers (including Moorhouses' Black Cat Mild, winner of the CAMRA National Championship in 2001) in traditional breweries that have been resurrected. Others such as Leyden (at The Lord Raglan, Nangreaves), Hart (Little Eccleston) and Porters (Haslingden) brew in and for their own pubs and an ever-expanding free trade. The future seems assured for these businesses, and you will find their products on sale in some of the pubs visited in this book.

Real Ale

Each of the pubs featured in this book has one thing in common: they all serve real ale on draught. In simple terms this means that the beers – milds, bitters, strong bitters, old ales and winter brews – are despatched "live" from the brewery whilst still fermenting; this secondary fermentation (so called because it supplements the primary fermentation which took place in the large brewing vessels at the brewery) continues slowly whilst the barrels are racked in the pub cellar or stillage. A spile hole allows the carbon dioxide produced by this action to escape. The matured beers are presented to the thirsty walker either direct from the barrel – a gravity-drawn beer – or via a hand-pump or electric pump attached to the bar. These pumping actions are the only extraneous pressures applied to the beers. Contrast this with the widely available and heavily advertised lagers and "smoothflow" beers which, although brewed in exactly the same manner and from the same raw ingredients as draught, are then pasteurised (i.e. the fermentation is killed off) and delivered in sealed, airtight kegs to pubs. The beer is then forced out of the kegs by introducing carbon dioxide (or nitrogen) under pressure into the keg; much of this gas dissolves in the pressurised liquid, resulting in the gassy beers and lagers familiar to many but shunned by lovers of traditional real ales.

Looking after traditional beer is a demanding job, the landlord/cellarman working to fine tolerances of temperature and cleanliness to ensure that the beer purchased is worthy of the name real ale. The "shelf-life" of draught beer is very short and the skill needed to keep a good pint is gained only by a combination of training and experience. Real ale pubs live or die largely on the reputation of the quality (or otherwise...) of the beer sold; whilst a publican can do nothing to alter the quality of a bad brew from a brewery, he/she can make all the difference between a passable pint and a great one. All the licensees featured in this book strive successfully to serve a great pint. If they don't – let them know: to you it's a bad pint, to them it could be the start of a slippery slope out of business.

Opening Hours

Under current legislation pubs in England can open for a maximum of twelve hours each day on Mondays to Saturdays (being 11 to 11) and between 12noon and 10.30pm on Sundays, unless local licensing magistrates have granted extensions. Many country pubs do not find it in their interest to take full advantage of these hours and tend to stick to the "traditional" hours of 12 to 3, and 6 to 11 or 7 to 11. Wherever possible I've indicated the opening hours of the pubs in this book as confirmed by the current licensee; these may vary from winter to summer so, if in doubt, give the pub a ring.

Since the new licensing laws introduced in the 1990's also encouraged (or, at least, allowed) licensees to apply for a "Child Licence", many pubs have become increasingly family-friendly, and young ramblers are now made welcome at many country pubs when accompanied by responsible adults. It is not possible to say with certainty which of the pubs featured in this book allow children on the premises as a change in licensee may mean a change in policy. Most, however, are understood to be child-friendly.

The Walks

Each of the walks in this book is believed to follow rights of way to which you, as a member of the public, has unrestricted access. Main and minor roads, by-ways, unadopted roads, towpaths, bridleways and public footpaths are all part of the Queen's Highway. In addition, there are concessionary and permissive footpaths, not strictly public footpaths but paths along which you have virtually unrestricted access. At the time of research and writing, all routes were free from any serious restriction or blockage (except where specified) but it is the nature of the animal that public rights of way, and public footpaths in particular, are prone to short-term changes due to repair work, agricultural practices, industrial development, road- and house-building schemes. It was a sad reflection on the state of England and Wales's 140,000 miles of public footpaths that a Countryside Commission survey carried out in 1990 suggested that your chances of completing even a modest countryside walk of only two miles without meeting access problems were a paltry one-in-three. The chances are not much better in 2002!

Definitive Rights of Way maps are prepared and maintained by staff employed by local authorities; the Ordnance Survey refer to these when updating and/or amending their series of maps. If you come across any problems on any of the walks in this book – or, indeed, on any other walk you undertake – and are certain that you are following a definitive right of way – you should initially approach the landowner to discuss the problem. More often than not this will be the local farmer; he or she is usually pleased to talk to ramblers – who are often the first to tell them of injured animals, damaged fences, etc. – and many maintain stiles of all descriptions to a high standard. If the problem is intractable, for example a wire fence, an impenetrable acreage of crops or a newly dug trout pond blocking the path, then you are quite within your rights to cross the fence or walk through the crops (or even swim the pond). Alternatively, in cases like this, you can try to follow the "line of least resistance" by circling a field or finding a handy farm gate; few farmers would object to you doing this although you have no legal right so to do. Unresolved problems should be reported to the Rights of Way Officer at the relevant District, Borough, Unitary or County Council. Problems encountered whilst walking in Country Parks should be reported to the Ranger service, usually on site; on canal towpaths to British Waterways and on National Trust land to the National Trust Regional Office.

None of the walks in this book is particularly strenuous and all should be easily completed by anyone of average fitness. You'll ob-

LOCATION MAP

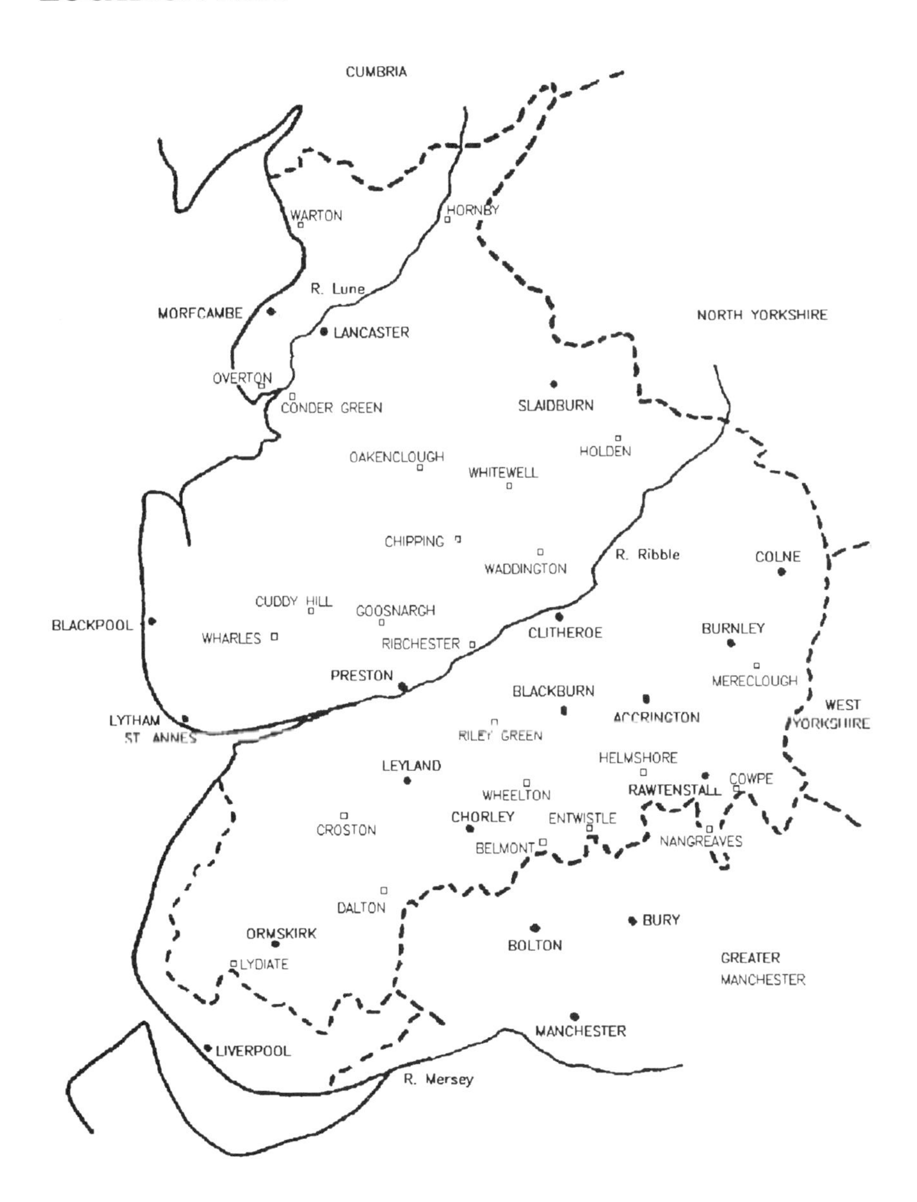

viously best know your own capabilities at walking but, as a rule of thumb, I'd suggest you allow a generous half an hour per mile for the walks; thus a six mile walk would take about three hours. This allows ample time for dawdling and sightseeing en route. Where particular problems do exist these are outlined in the text or highlighted at the beginning of each walk description. As for clothing, a good, comfortable, waterproof pair of boots is essential; I, personally, would not countenance wellingtons as being ideal although some renowned walkers do swear by them. The rest is just common sense and largely dictatable by the weather, but do remember that, even at a height of only a few hundred feet, winds can be chilly and showers can develop virtually out of nothing, so always carry a windproof, waterproof jacket and a sweater.

The walks are grouped into generalised geographical areas, some of which are necessarily large so that all walks in one area may not be particularly contiguous. A description of each area is given in the introductory passage of the first walk in each section; the reference number of the relevant Ordnance Survey Explorer Series sheet(s) is given in the titles of each walk. You should have no problems in doing the walks using the sketch maps and the directions in the text, but it is always useful to have the wider perspective offered by an Ordnance Survey map to identify features of interest or to plan an alternative route should the need arise.

1. The West Pennines: Entwistle

Route: Entwistle – Wayoh Reservoir – Turton Tower – Jumbles Country Park – Affetside – Hawkshaw – Edgworth

Distance: Either 11 miles or 5 miles

Map: Explorer 287 West Pennine Moors

Start: The Strawbury Duck, Entwistle

Access: The best way to get to and from this walk is by rail. Entwistle station, on the Manchester Victoria to Blackburn line, is virtually next door to the pub. Trains run regularly, Mondays to Saturdays, early morning to late evening, and two hourly on Sundays after midday (timetable enquiries 08457 484950). If travelling by car take the A676 road from Bolton towards Burnley. About 3 miles out of Bolton, at the village of Walves, look for the Bulls Head on your left, at a sharp corner; turn left here and drive to Edgworth. Go straight over the junction here towards Darwen. Pass the red-brick chapel on your left then look for the very narrow Hob Lane, also on the left (there's a signpost opposite pointing the way to Entwistle and the Strawbury Duck). Follow Hob Lane to its end, crossing the reservoir en route. The pub is just over the railway bridge; parking is restricted.

The Strawbury Duck (01204 852013)

When you're doing one of the other walks in this book ask any other walker you happen upon if they've been to the Strawbury Duck. Chances are that the answer will be in the affirmative as the pub is a veritable institution amongst the walking fraternity of the North West. Slap-bang in the middle of the West Pennine Moors Recreational Area and with views stretching forever, the pub is the ideal spot to relax on a summer's evening after a long walk – or on a winter weekend day after a shorter ramble over the frost- and snow-crisped moorland.

Aside from its location, the top attraction of the Strawbury Duck is the range of beers kept by landlord and proprietors Roger and Lisa Boardman. The bar and side-hatch bristle with handpumps. At few places will you find a better pint of Black Sheep or Timothy Taylor's

Landlord, these being complemented by a variety of 100 guest beers, of which four different ones are served every week. If you are there in the depths of winter, you will also usually find a barrel of monumentally strong winter ale on stillage behind the bar and a powerful home-concocted mulled wine. The Duck is also widely renowned for its superb range of home-cooked food.

The pub was originally called The Station Hotel (no prizes....) and owned by the now-defunct Duttons brewery. Twice they tried to close the pub in 1965 and 1970, but each time the axe failed to fall. After the second time, it became a free house and acquired the unusual name. Locals had long known it as the Strawberry due to the colour of the stonework in the setting sun. It is now painted black and white. The owner of the new free house freely adapted this name, changing the berry to bury after the town a few miles away and adding duck as a variation of his own surname, Duxbury, hence Strawbury Duck. The name stuck and this idiosyncratic whim became part of ramblers' folklore.

A warren of small rooms and nooks radiates from the bar area, generally stone-slabbed with beamed ceilings and warmed by open log fires. Half of the pub is the old Station Hotel, about a century old, the other half was added in 1981 with the addition of the adjoining 300-year-old cottage. It is very much of a family pub and is open all day: Mon-Sat, noon – 11pm; Sun, noon – 10.30pm. Food is served Mon-Sat, noon – 9.30pm; Sun, noon – 8pm.

The West Pennine Moors

Rambling along on either of the two walks in this chapter you're right in the heart of The West Pennine Moors, a distinct bloc of the Pennine chain bounded to the north by the River Darwen and to the south by the "mill towns" of Bolton and Bury. The area is characterised by high moorland tracts – some of the highest land in Lancashire – deep wooded cloughs, eerie remains of long-abandoned quarries and a plethora of lakes. These latter features are all artificial, the more than generous rainfall of the area stored up to slake the thirst of Liverpudlians, Boltonians and Buryites. The largest and most spectacular are those in the far west at Anglezarke and Rivington, nearly 150 years old; the most picturesque are those visited on this walk in the twin valleys of the Bradshaw and Broadhead Brooks.

Prior to flooding, these same valleys saw the birth of the industrial revolution; farmers doubling as weavers processing local wool used the power of the streams to drive simple machinery and the water to wash, shrink and bleach the product. Production of fustian, a mix of cotton fibres and linen, was also important by the 1600s, only in the 19th century did the familiar cotton towns develop from this Tudor base. Many of the dour, mullioned gritstone manor houses that still dot the area – Entwistle Old Hall for example – and the small "Folds" of cottages came about thanks to the wealth generated from this embryonic industrial revolution.

The Walk

Two walks are suggested in this area, both have a common first two miles and final mile. From the pub, cross the railway bridge and follow the road downhill. Having passed the breezeblock stables on your left, turn right up the track opposite a lamppost and walk up between a barn and Entwistle Old Hall. Just past the barn, look for a stile on the left, cross it and walk ahead across the small pasture to the stone-slab stile. Pass through this and walk across the field ahead, reaching the far side about 30 yards up from the row of cottages. Wind through the gaps in the barbed wire, looking to your right for a short walled path leading up to a stile. Climb this stile (by a waymark signpost) and turn left to a further stile. Once over this descend the steps and follow the path as it winds right, sinking deeply between high, tree-lined banks. At the end, the path issues onto a causeway across an arm of Wayoh Reservoir. To your right, the Bolton-Blackburn railway crosses the drowned Armsgrove Clough on its sombre viaduct, to your left drink in the extensive views over to Holcombe Moor and Harcles Hill. Wildfowl on the reservoir include great crested grebe, a multitude of species of duck and the ubiquitous heron and kingfisher.

At the end of the causeway leave the main path and go straight ahead up the narrow path with the tiny clough to your immediate right. Pass through the stile at the top and walk along the partly paved path to reach the drive to Armsgrove Farm. Continue ahead along this and at the end turn right to enter the tiny fold of cottages. Walk along past these solid old cottages and the parsonage, bear right along past the Cupressus hedge and walk to Greens Arms Road. Here turn right and cross the railway bridge, then walk straight

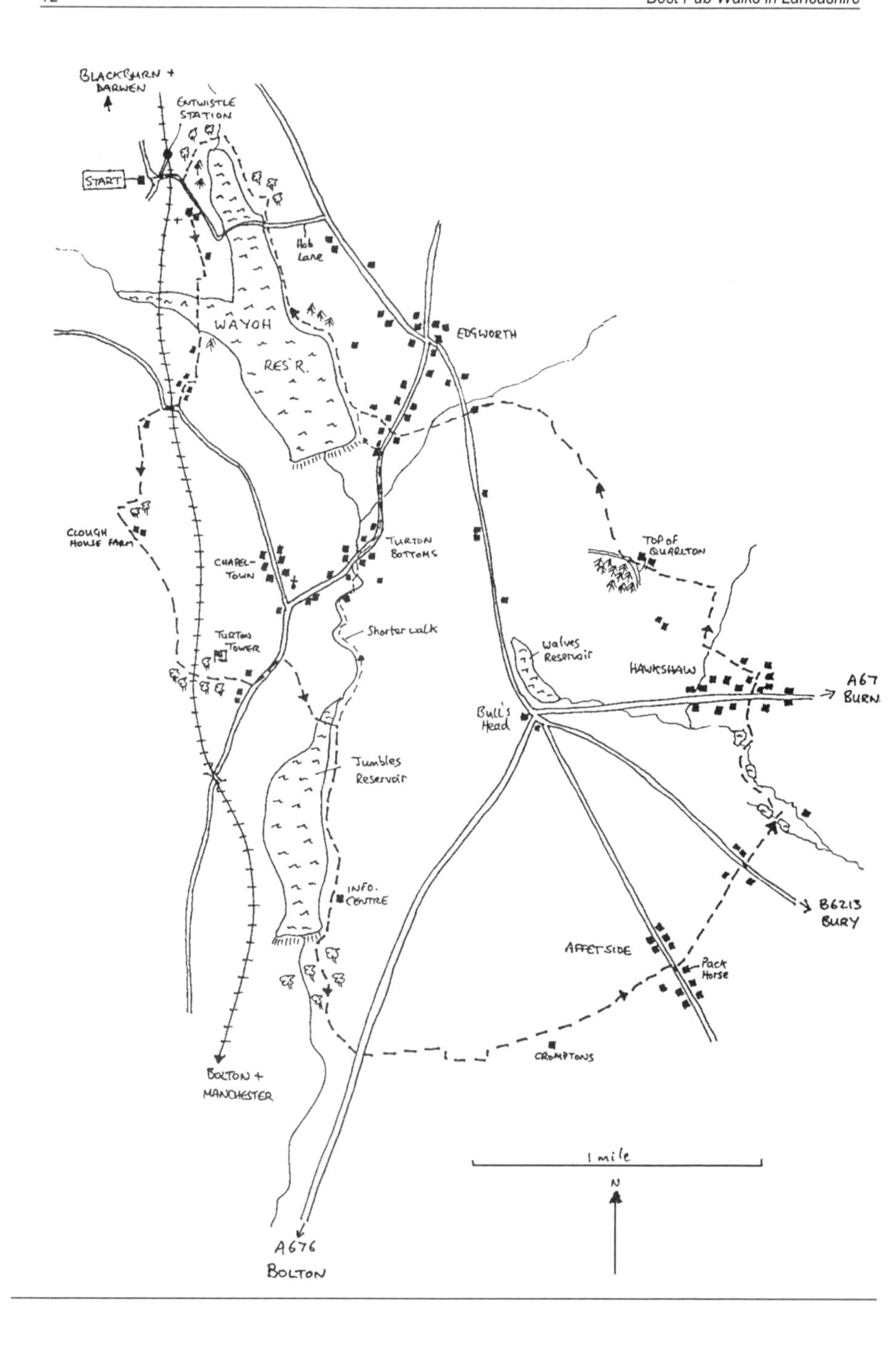
BLACKBURN + DARWEN
ENTWISTLE STATION
START
Hob Lane
WAYOH RES'R.
EDGWORTH
CLOUGH HOUSE FARM
CHAPEL-TOWN
TURTON BOTTOMS
TOP OF QUARLTON
Shorter walk
TURTON TOWER
Walves Reservoir
HAWKSHAW
A67 BURN
Bull's Head
Jumbles Reservoir
INFO. CENTRE
B6213 BURY
AFFETSIDE
Pack Horse
CROMPTONS
BOLTON + MANCHESTER
1 mile
N
A676 BOLTON

ahead along the drive to Lowes Moor. Stick with the drive as it passes to the right of the small Georgian mansion, curve round behind the redeveloped barn and go through the tall gate to the left of the farm gate. Cross the brook, then the stile to the right of the next gate and walk up to the right along the field edge. From the next stile, look for the line of trees ahead – the ones with the buildings peeking through – and cross the rough pasture to these, fording a narrow clough en route. On reaching the wall this side of the trees, turn right and walk up to the surfaced moorland road, turning left along this and cross the cattle grid.

Turton Tower

Pass by Clough House Farm, where there are some peculiar octagonal brick towers, and follow the track along keeping the wall to your immediate left and ignoring any tracks off to the right. The rounded moorland top on your right is Cheetham Close on top of which are the scant remains of a stone circle. Pass through the gate-stile at the end of the track and head left along the track, down the wooded clough. At the end of this, you should cross the railway on the castellated folly bridge, built to mirror nearby Turton Tower for the owner at the time, James

Kay, a noted local industrialist and director of the railway company. Continuing downhill, Turton Tower comes into view on your left. It is said to be a pele tower (more common in Northumberland and the northern Lakes) with Elizabethan "magpie" additions. Inside is an Aladdin's cave of armour, medieval weaponry and Tudor furniture and a remarkable chandelier made from stags' antlers. The hall belongs to Blackburn Council and is open to the public (phone 01204 852203 for details).

Walk down to the main road and turn left, then at the bottom of the slope take the signposted path off to the right, which leads past the pillbox. Pass by the pond at the crest of the hill and enter the woodland beyond, following the path through the trees to emerge at a bridge across the top end of Jumbles Reservoir. Cross this bridge. It is at this point that the shorter and longer walks diverge.

Shorter Walk

Once across this bridge turn left and walk along the path beside the reservoir, which soon peters out to become the feeder brook, Bradshaw Brook. Simply remain with the path and pass the terrace of three-storey houses to reach a factory car park. Bear left across the bridge out of the car park and walk up to the main road in this, the hamlet of Turton Bottoms. When you reach the road turn right and walk steeply uphill to reach the Black Bull pub, from beside which a footpath leads to the eastern bank of Wayoh Reservoir. Walk up along this path, which here rejoins the route of the longer walk (now go to the final paragraph).

Longer Walk

Turn right off the bridge and walk along the path that skirts the reservoir. Much of this bank is a nature reserve, so observe the restriction notices. After a while the path climbs away from the reservoir and reaches the information centre for Jumbles Country Park (open Easter to October on Wednesday, Saturday, Sunday and Bank Holiday afternoons and on Sunday afternoons only during the winter). Beyond this is the warden's office and large car park. Aim for the far right-hand corner of this car park and walk down the steps, turning right at the bottom. In a matter of 20 or so yards bear left and follow the path up the hillside through the oak woodlands, an old mill leat gradually falling away to your right. Cross the stile beside the gate and walk up along the track to the main road.

Cross straight over and take the tarred lane opposite. This roughens as it rises up the ridge, skirting a covered reservoir (left) to reach the yard at Crompton's Farm. Climb the stile immediately left of this yard. Your way now lies straight ahead along a track partially infilled with rubble; aim to walk along the line of pylons. There are good views from this point; Darwen's Jubilee Tower and Bolton's Town Hall are easily discernible landmarks. Where the infill ends just carry straight on up the field, cross the stile at the end and walk up to the road at the hamlet of Affetside. This is the line of the Roman road between Manchester and Ribchester. Turning right brings you almost immediately to The Pack Horse Inn, another favourite haunt of local ramblers and rambling clubs and offering hand-pumped Hydes' ales.

Thirst quenched, take the path that goes to the left of the pub and alongside the car park; it soon becomes a walled pathway leading down off the ridge. Directly ahead is the second of Lancashire's famous three towers, Peel's Monument, high above Ramsbottom. The extensive views from here also include the flat-topped Knowle Hill, Saddleworth Moor and the Dark Peak. Remain with this path, pass by the house to your left and walk down to the minor road. Here turn right and walk to the telephone box just beyond the cottages. Turn left here at the footpath sign, cross the stile at the end of the garden and walk down the field with the hedge to your right.

Cross the stile at the foot of the pasture and walk across the dam between the two mill lodges. Bear right at the far end of this dam and walk down a few stone steps to the thorn bush, turning left at this point to gradually descend the hillside along the widest green track, and walking in the general direction of a white-painted house on the hillside ahead. Stick with the path, passing below a chimneystack and above the remains of a mill. At one point, you have to ford a shallow stream. Up to the left here is a waterfall, well hidden in a wooded cleft in the hillside. Keep along the level path past the waymark post, passing above further reedy lodges. Keep right at the fork beyond these to a stile and gate. Turn right along the rough lane and then go left at the cross-lanes in 40 paces, rising to the main street in Hawkshaw.

Cross straight over and walk up Hawkshaw Lane. In about 200 yards, you reach Tonge Fold Cottage on your right. On your left at this point a public footpath sign points the way along a driveway. Go along here for about 40 yards and angle left along the narrow path just before the garage – there's a footpath sign pointing the way. Pass through the stile at the end and walk ahead down across the pasture to the drive. Cross the stile here and then turn right and walk across the bridge, remaining with the gently rising track for several hundred yards. At the point where the lone wooden post stands to your right, look up left to sight the line of an old wall up the hillside (if you've reached the lone thorn bush you've gone too far) and walk up the line of this wall to the stile at the crest. Cross this and walk uphill to the barn adjoining Top of Quarlton Farm.

Go across the stile to the left of the gate on the left of the barn and walk to the farm drive. Look half-left here to find a waymark arrow directing you up the outside of the farmhouse's garden. Walk up beside this wall and then several yards of wooden rail fencing to a wide stile immediately before the metal gate on your right and at a bend in the track; there's a plantation of fir trees on your left. Cross this, walk ahead to the cross fence and turn left to the stile in the corner. Cross this and walk to the corner of the wire fence, then bear half-right and walk down across the field to a further stile a few yards from the field corner. Once over this follow the path ahead, remaining some way above the floor of the shallow valley down to your right. Keep your eyes on the fence in the valley, however, and when you see the waymark arrow, cross this fence and walk to the left along the embankment. You'll have to leave this to go through the wire fence that cuts this embankment (gate to your left) but regain it and walk to its end.

Cross the rough track and walk ahead across the pasture, looking for a frame stile at the far side, just beyond the row of thorn trees. Once over this, head down across the next field aiming for the corner of the wall pointing directly at you. At this corner is a stone slab stile through which you should pass, then follow the line of the fence on your right down to the stream. Turn downstream and look for the stile on the far bank, reaching this via the large boulders in the stream. Once over the stile climb up to the path and turn left to reach a road at a gateway some yards above a new house.

Turn left along the road and cross it, soon passing the Edgworth village nameplate. About 100 yards past this take the kissing gate on the right, following the path down to a stile into a woodland path. Cross the stone footbridge and then turn left to and through the kissing gate. At the wooden footbridge, don't cross this but, rather, angle half-right up the steep field, an occasionally boggy path leading to a redundant mid-field gate. Pass by this, keeping below the house. Bend round with the far end of the wall to find a kissing gate by a field gate; beyond this take the cobbled lane, then rough road up through Brandwood Fold to the main road. Cross this and turn left, then turn up along Harbour Lane. Walk along to the end of Harbour Lane and cross the waymarked stile that is immediately to the right of the drive of the last house on the left. Walk on to a further stile a matter of yards away, cross this and walk ahead to the path alongside Wayoh Reservoir, turning right along this, waymarked as the Witton Weavers Way. The name "Wayoh" is derived from the Old English words for "path along a ridge."

From this point (where the shorter walk rejoins) remain with the path up along this eastern bank of the reservoir. Cross over the narrow road (Hob Lane) and continue through the trees, the reservoir gradually becoming reedy and silted off to your left. When you reach the green-based footbridge over Broadhead Brook cross it and walk along the track ahead, shortly coming to another footbridge, which you should also cross. From here walk straight ahead and take the left-hand path of the two that go up the hillside in front of you (i.e. the one without the stile). Follow this path up through the trees to a stile, cross this and then climb the steep pasture to another stile. Go over this and walk uphill along the road back to the pub.

2. The West Pennines: Helmshore

Route: Helmshore – Grane Valley – Haslingden Grane – Windy Harbour

Distance: 6.5 miles

Map: Explorer 287 West Pennine Moors

Start: The Robin Hood, Helmshore

Access: Helmshore is one mile south of Haslingden on the B6214 road to Bury. The Robin Hood is on the B6235 Holcombe Road, about 150 yards north of the Helmshore Textile Museums; the easiest thing is to follow the brown road signs to the Museums which are well signposted locally and from the main A56 dual carriageway.

The Robin Hood (01706 213180)

Remember Adam Adamant? The be-swordsticked Victorian detective frozen in a block of ice by fiendish Chinese villains only to be thawed out in 1960s London. If he'd thawed out in The Robin Hood in 2001 he'd feel immediately at home as the pub has been as if in amber since it first became a licensed premises in the 1880s. It's as unspoilt a pub as you'll find anywhere.

It would be easy to overlook the tiny roadside pub nestling in the narrow gorge of the Ogden Brook, one blink and you'd have passed it by. The small bar serves three interconnecting rooms hollowed out of this ground floor of the two mill-workers cottages it once was. Open fires warm tiny rooms decorated with watercolours, brasses, prints, mill shuttles, an old cornet and – as you can't fail to notice – ducks. Landlord Colin Ruleman obviously has a thing about our aquatic feathered friends; there are brass ducks and porcelain ducks, pot ducks and wicker ducks, flying ducks and prints of ducks. Even the ends of the seat in front of the pub are duck shaped. And if you look out of the windows at the side or back you'll see the real thing on the Ogden Brook or one of the millponds that the pub overlooks. The nearest pond has been stocked with goldfish and Koi carp which may be immune to ducks but not to the heron or kingfishers which you can watch from the windows or from the tiny beer garden that hangs precariously high over the water.

These ponds and the river, together with the steep, tree-lined slope beyond, give the pub an enviable position in this old established industrial area; Higher Mill and Whittaker's Mill (which the ponds serve) look nothing less than picturesque, a rare accolade for such "Dark Satanic" buildings. To help you enjoy the setting is an excellently kept pint of hand-pumped Tetley's Bitter, Phoenix or Moorhouses – ignore the Wilson's sign outside, it's just another anachronism. Four different guest beers are served each week out of 100 regularly sourced. The pub also keeps spirits. Or at least one, the ghost of an old mill worker christened Wilf. As many as forty people used to live in the cottages before the pub was developed and Wilf is finding it impossible to leave. Perhaps he likes the beer (Colin Ruleman has had pint pots mysteriously move about the pub overnight) or the regular live music sessions, usually folk, jazz or Cajun). Even an exorcism in the 1980's failed to persuade the ghost to leave, Colin's dog certainly still senses a presence from time to time although Colin himself has yet to achieve a sighting.

The Robin Hood is open between 4.00pm and 11.00pm on Mondays to Fridays, from 1.00pm to 11.00pm on Saturdays and 1.00pm to 10.30pm on Sundays. There's no food, but the pub boasts two welcoming log fires and was winner of the CAMRA "Pub of the Year, East Lancashire" in 2001.

Helmshore Textile Museums

Two adjoining but unconnected old mills are now the focal point of this, the major working museum of Lancashire's textile and weaving heritage. Higher Mill, the older of the two mills and built in 1789, is a woollen fulling mill complete with fully operational fulling stocks powered by a waterwheel. The wheel is fed from the long, narrow millpond above the mill in the deep, winding gorge of the Ogden Brook. Fulling was the process by which loosely woven fabrics were converted into tightly knitted cloth, the broadcloth that was the staple material on which the whole of the vast woollen textile industry of Lancashire was based. The initial loose fabric was soaked in water, impregnated with fuller's earth to disperse unwanted natural oils and then hammered flat on the fulling stocks. The mill last worked commercially in 1967 and much restoration work, including a rebuilding of the waterwheel in 1978, has produced a fine live museum. Higher Mill also houses the leading collection of early carding and spinning machines including a spinning jenny and an Arkwright's water frame.

The adjoining Whittaker's Mill is a Victorian cotton-spinning mill that used a steam powered condenser system to convert cotton waste into material such as flannelette, its last productive year was 1978. This is the major part of the museum housing a comprehensive history of the Lancashire wool, cotton and flax industries, with working spinning mules and carding engines taking up virtually the whole of one floor. Opening hours vary through the year, for details telephone 01706 226459.

The Grane Valley

It's hard to believe but only a century ago this quiet, virtually deserted valley was a hive of activity with weaving, quarrying, farming and even illegal whisky distilling keeping well over 1000 folk occupied in a thriving upland community. The rise of the factory system put paid to the weaving, economics saw off most of the farming families and all but two of the quarries. Whatever happened to the illegal stills? The thirst for water to satisfy the burgeoning population and industries of Bury, nine miles to the south, also played its part with a string of reservoirs being created between 1850 and 1912 drowning productive pastureland. Probably only a couple of dozen people now live in the valley, littered with gaunt ruins of farmhouses and cottages, eerie wastes of long abandoned and overgrown quarries and criss-crossed by half-forgotten moorland roads, tracks and paths. The information centre at Clough Head Quarry, just off the route of the walk and accessible via a short link path, is the place to visit to gain greater insight into this fascinating, little known corner of Lancashire. It is open between Easter and October on Saturday, Sunday and Bank Holiday afternoons; rest of the year, Sundays only.

The Walk

Go uphill from the Robin Hood, the river and millpond down to your right, overshadowed by the viaduct of the long dead railway. Pass a small terrace of cottages on your right and a second terrace on your left. Immediately past this second terrace, a public footpath sign directs you up the track behind the houses towards Musbury Heights. Walk up this, bear right at the fork and cross the stile by the gate. Continue uphill, bear right at the top to pass between a barn and a ruined house, walking on to the end of the track. The distinctive "Table Mountain" hill on the left is Tor Hill. Cross the stile at the end and turn right up the rutted track, shortly passing by the ivy-covered gable of the old farm on your right. Go straight ahead up the hedged track, crossing two stiles, over the bank at the end and straight ahead up the field road. Pass through the gate at the end, walk up to the fork and bear right, following the rough track around the snout of the hill.

Walk round the corner, the views opening out eastwards over Holden Wood Reservoir, ignoring the first turn right. At the second turn, no more than a large gap in the wall and bank, bear right and look for the stile just to the right of two small thorn bushes below you. Cross this and look for the ladder stile down to your left. Follow the line of the stream down, walk behind the rebuilt house and cross the stile, then the ladder stile. Turn left and follow the line of broken wall and fence along the hillside, working your way gradually downhill to reach the wooden gate and rail fencing, beside which is a stile to cross. From here walk ahead along the well-maintained footpath, passing by the foot of an old incline which once carried wagons bearing gritstone blocks and flagstones down from the huge quarries on Musbury Heights, far up to your left.

With Ogden Reservoir to your right, wind along with the path, gradually working uphill to pass round the top of a deeply incised clough. Bear right here, ignoring the concessionary path off to the left (which leads up to the old quarry workings, a worthwhile detour if you have time) and contour along the path for a further half-mile or so. Pass by the isolated tree, above the dam of Calf Hey Reservoir; continue for about 100 yards, then follow the waymark arrow along the lower path. This is part of the Rossendale Way, a waymarked route that offers a long circuit of the Borough of Rossendale.

Just before the woodland, cross the slatted wooden footbridge and climb the steps, zig-zagging round and over the two stiles to join the path across the top of the woods. Cross a further board footbridge, climb the steps and then turn left along the path at the top. Follow this along and over a further footbridge hidden in a deep clough, then walk along for about 60 yards to the point where the path bends left and passes a final tree on the right. Just beyond this point, and before you reach the old stone gateposts, a waymark post off to your left marks your route. Simply follow the waymarks up the hillside to end up at the top corner of the plantation of conifers.

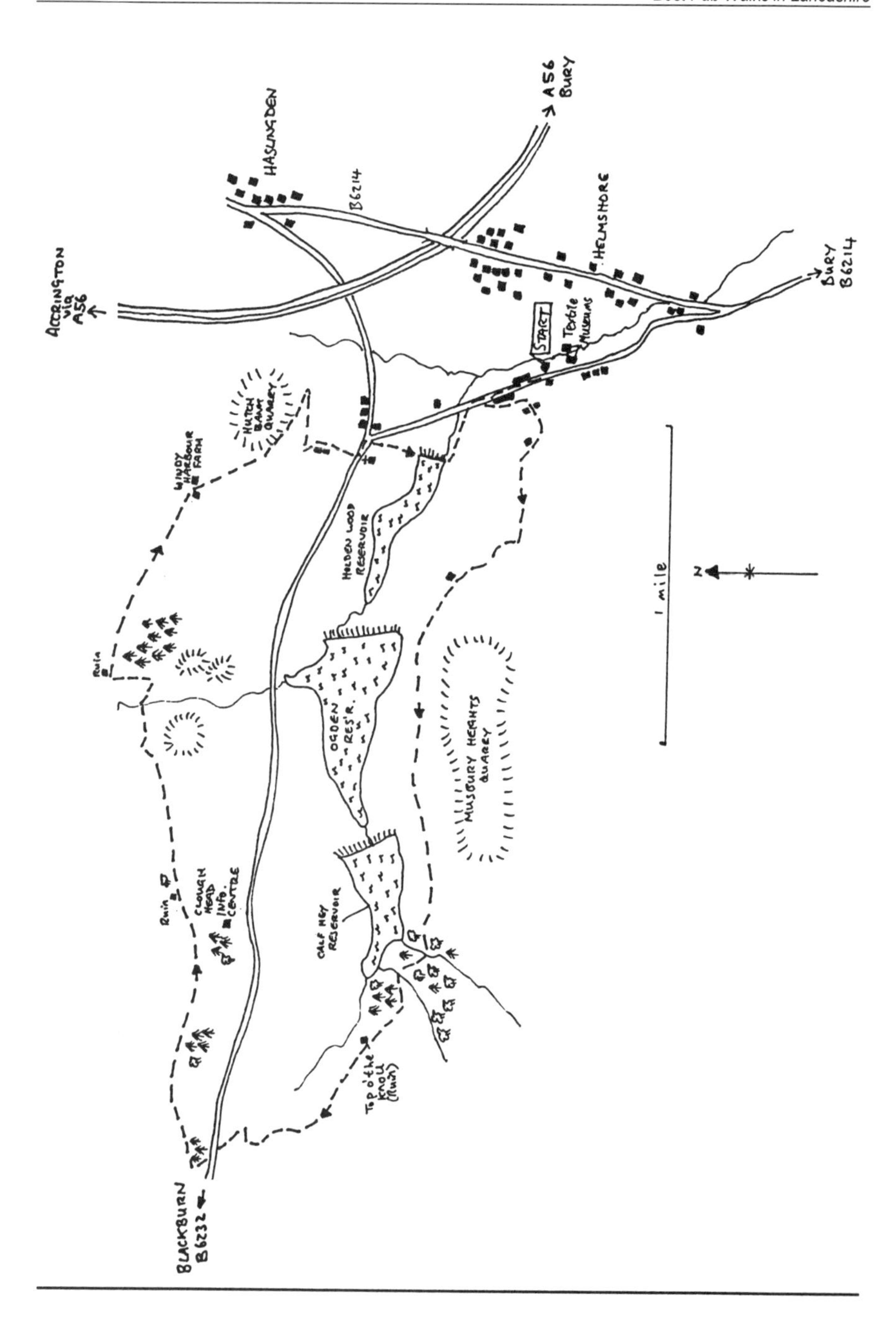
A56 BURY
HASLINGDEN
B6214
HELMSHORE
BURY B6214
ACCRINGTON via A56
START
Textile Museums
HUTCH BANK QUARRY
WINDY HARBOUR FARM
HOLDEN WOOD RESERVOIR
1 mile
N
Ruin
OGDEN RES'R.
MUSBURY HEIGHTS QUARRY
Ruin
CLOUGH HEAD INFO. CENTRE
CALF HEY RESERVOIR
Top o' th' Knoll (Ruin)
BLACKBURN B6232

From here continue as indicated by the waymarkers, crossing stiles as necessary to end up at the substantial ruins of Top o' th' Knoll Farm. Work your way round the left-hand side of these and follow the track across the hillside beyond.

Remain with this old, walled, in places paved track, passing several more ruins to reach a small waterfall down to your right. Beyond this, the route of the track is barred by a wall between two gateposts. Cross the stream and track at this point and then continue to follow its line, keeping it just to your left until past the boggy section. Walk along for about 400 yards and then bear right with the hairpin. A few yards on follow the direction of the waymark to the left, walk up across the field and climb the stile to gain the main road – just head for the left-hand corner of the small plantation on the hillside. Cross straight over the road and follow the rough track and stream up beside the trees. At the top climb the rickety stile and turn right.

For the next two miles, the route of the walk is alongside the wall to your right, crossing stiles as necessary. In a mile or so you'll see Clough Head Quarry car park and information centre down to your right; should you wish to visit this, the path to it is waymarked from a point immediately before the isolated group of trees you reach. Pass the trees and a working quarry soon becomes visible off to the right. You should remain well up from this, following the occasional yellow waymark arrow. In a short while walk downhill to pass along the embankment above an abandoned quarry site. Cross the stream and climb the steep clough side, aiming for the ruins by the lone tree, near to which is a waymarker directing you straight ahead.

After a short distance go through the gap in the wall by the waymark arrow and aim for the bottom right-hand corner of the field, from where a further waymarker on a post directs you to some trees by a ruin. Walk to the moorland road here and turn left, walking uphill for about 150 yards to the tree beside the gate on your right. Climb the stile and walk along the track through the old gateposts, following the wall on your right. Keep to the left of the tall wall you come to and go through the gate, following the track along until you reach Windy Harbour Farm. Pass the first barn and then turn right, go through the yard gate and walk along the track past a further barn and away from the farm. At the end of this track go through the gate ahead and follow the track around the lip of the quarry.

This large quarry, Hutch Bank, is still working, but you see little

Higher Mill (left) and Whitaker's Mill, Helmshore

despite its proximity. What you do get is enormous views in virtually every direction. Walk gradually downhill with the track to the point where the fence falls away to the right and the road curves away to the left. Fall along with the fence to reach a very precarious stile on your right. Cross this and walk along the old track, climb over a gate and continue downhill. At the bottom, the track meets another at a very sharp angle. Turn sharp left here and then in a matter of yards climb the bank on your right to the corner of a wall. From here sight the white painted cottage below you and walk to it, go down the track beside it, pass through the gap stile at the end and walk on down to the main road.

Cross the road and turn left, passing by the church to reach the hamlet of Holden Wood. Turn right down the road towards Helmshore and then immediately past the Holden Arms pub car park turn right along the narrow road to Holden Wood Reservoir. Cross the dam and bear right. Immediately on your left take the path up behind the retaining wall and follow the line of fence on your right. As this ends, walk ahead along the path which descends through an area of scrubby woodland to the road at the bottom. Turn right along this to return to the Robin Hood.

3. The West Pennines: Belmont

Route: Belmont – Longworth Clough – Dimple – Longworth Moor

Distance: 7 miles

Map: Explorer 287 West Pennine Moors

Start: The Black Dog, Belmont, Bolton

Access: Belmont village is some 5 miles north of Bolton on the A675 road to Preston. The Black Dog is on the left about 200 yards after the sharp bend that heralds the village. The entrance to the car park is off the minor road signposted to Rivington, the pub itself is on the corner of this road and the A675.

The Black Dog (01204 811218)

This is the northernmost pub in the tied estate of the small Manchester family brewery of Joseph Holt; in all they have only just over one hundred pubs. These choice beers, which have a fanatical following, are nationally renowned as being amongst the cheapest in Britain. The bitter is famously very bitter, the mild very dark and slightly fruity; both are kept particularly well in this moorland edge pub.

The Black Dog was built as a farmhouse in the 1750s. In 1825, the middle part of the farm was converted into a pub and it remained a farm-cum-pub until the 1930s, beer was brewed on site until the late-1920s. In 1952, Holts purchased the pub from the local butcher. During the 19th century, the village court was held in what is now the snug, directly opposite the bar. The jurors' benches remain set into the walls of this tiny area, the local squire, also the magistrate for the area, sat at the end of the bench distinguished by an additional armrest.

The pub has a connection with a famous local murder. In 1838 a Scottish peddler named George Henderson, who lived locally, had made his regular walk across nearby Winter Hill from the Horwich side to the Black Dog. En route back to Horwich he was waylaid and murdered high on the lonely moors; the site on Winter Hill is marked by a plaque and simple monument known as Scotchman's Stump.

Every available beam in the pub is festooned with old pewter tankards and pint pots, steins and Toby jugs; there is even a potty (possibly a variation on a yard of ale?). The walls are crammed full of framed prints and old photographs and every nook and cranny (of which there are legion) houses an oddment or artefact. If all this sounds rather kitsch, it is not – the building was seemingly built specifically to house such ornamentation.

The manager, Heino Chrobok, previously from 'The Globe' in nearby Egerton, has established a reputation for excellent pub meals – chilli, steak and kidney pie, chicken curry – all home-cooked. An enormous collection of classical and contemporary music tapes provides background music throughout the day, often drowned out by the idle chatter of both locals, and ramblers who ensure the pub always has a lively atmosphere. The pub has a large function room, which is regularly used by such as the local hang-gliding club (Winter Hill is renowned as a hang-gliding location despite the television mast) and the potholing, fly-fishers and caving club. The classical music theme is occasionally picked up in all-but impromptu concerts given by a 10-piece (or more) orchestra made up of members of the Hallé, the Northern Chamber Orchestra and other internationally known musicians – all for fun and to benefit local charities.

The Black Dog is open Mon-Sat, noon – 11pm; Sun, noon – 10.30pm. Bar meals are available daily from noon – 2pm; Wed-Sat, 6.00 – 8.00pm and Sun, noon – 3.00pm and 6.30 to 8.00pm. Children are welcome, and if you want to discover the West Pennines in depth you can stay at the pub – the old stables have been converted into three letting rooms.

Belmont

This is a small moorland village about 850ft above sea level straggling up the northern bank of the Horden Brook. The original hamlet was called Horden but was renamed in about 1800 by the owner and developer of the calico and print works that gave rise to much of the housing in the village. Maria Square, opposite the pub car park, was built first in 1804, soon followed by piecemeal developments of tiny squares and terraces, some of the latter built on a hillside so steep that they have two storeys at the front but four at the rear. The calico

The Black Dog, Belmont

works closed in the 1860's but a dye and bleach works opened soon afterwards and this remains in operation today, its chimney a local landmark. The village is dominated by the brooding mass of Winter Hill, at around 1500ft the highest point in the West Pennines area and itself capped by a giant television transmitter mast.

The Walk

From the pub car park cross the main road and walk down the street known as Maria Square. The green to the right will often be bustling with dozens of ducks, which alternatively use the old lodges visible to the left at the bottom end of the Square. At the foot of the hill, carry straight on along the road through the dyeing and bleaching works and uphill beyond. Shortly after you have passed the two cottages on your right is a walled enclosure and parking spot, also on the right. Immediately before this is a stone step stile into the pasture. Walk down this pasture, cross the stile at the bottom and walk across the long wooden footbridge, closely followed by the dam that holds back an "Ornamental Reservoir."

Turn left at the end of the dam and follow the course of the mill leat on your right, remaining with this for the best part of a mile. A little way along a series of waterfalls lie well hidden down to the left in the deep wooded clough of Horden Brook. In the summer months, the path is lined with a veritable forest of Himalayan balsam and the leat is a popular fishing ground with heron and kingfisher.

Walk around the hillside with the leat and then a few yards beyond to reach the farm road. Keep left along this to reach the entrance to a fold of renovated houses and a three-way fingerpost. Turn left here, taking the path nearest to the wall, soon crossing a short section of boardwalk. Pass through the kissing gate at the corner and take the long series of railed steps down to gain a path beside Horden Brook, flowing now through the wooded Longworth Clough. This is a nature reserve managed by the local Wildlife Trust. Follow this downstream, ignoring the footbridge you soon reach on your left. This path winds through unimproved meadowland rich in wildflowers, rising beneath a set of electricity cables to the far bottom end of a paper mill complex. From here, the path is obvious, leading down away from the factory and into the woodlands. Locally, walkers have forged an unofficial alternative route below the mill to regain the right of way, some way downstream. Just follow the waymarks.

Walk down through the woods and then alongside the stream, crossing this via the wooden footbridge several hundred yards downstream. Once on the opposite bank bear right and follow the wide path down along the field. Where this path splits at a stone bridge bear left (don't cross the bridge) and then very shortly left again at the end of the fence, scrambling up the slope to the stile. Cross this and follow the fence on your left up to the next stile, from here aiming for the left of Higher Critchley Fold Farm. Pass through the gap stile in the wall, turn left and left again along the minor road. Follow this for several hundred yards to the grassy face of Delph Reservoir's dam, whereupon turn right along the path at the foot of this slope.

The path leads across a massive stone footbridge over the outflow stream from the reservoir and up a walled track to the hamlet of Dimple. At the end of this track, you reach a small chapel and school on your left. The chapel is Walmersley Unitarian Chapel and dates from 1713. The inside is a delight with wooden box pews and a large wooden balcony around three walls; if it is locked you can see well

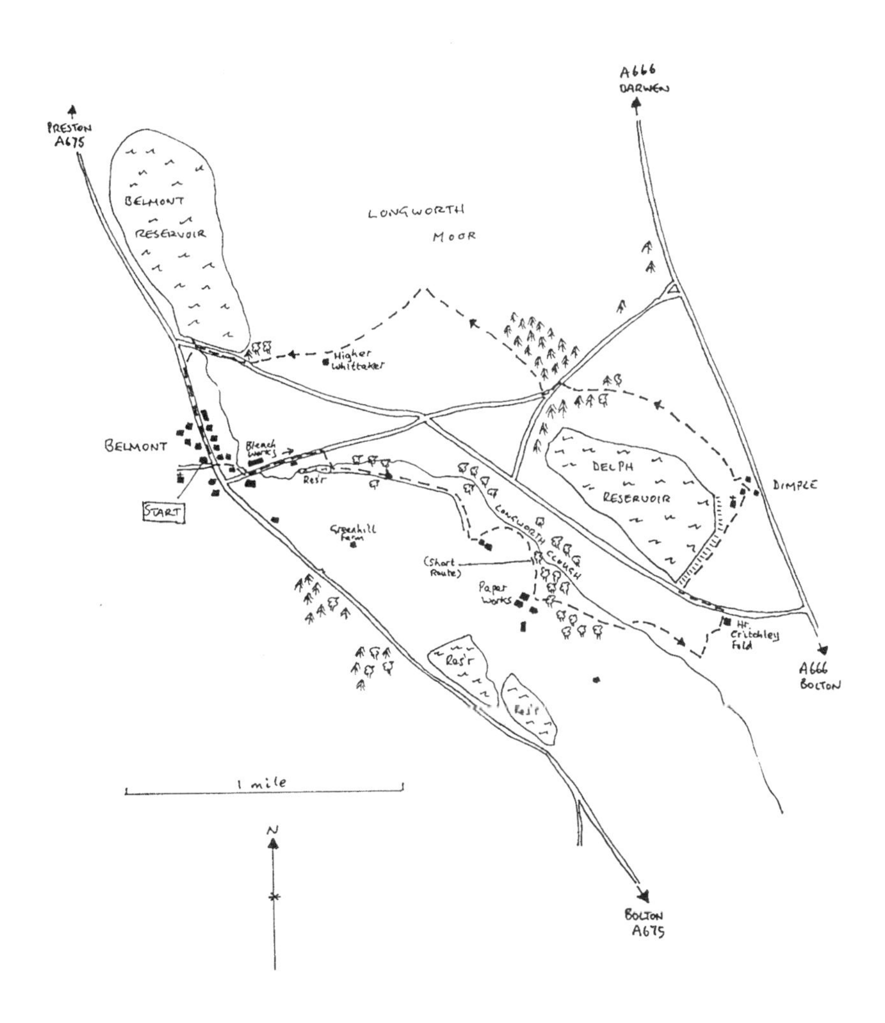

enough through the windows. The adjoining school dates from 1851.

Walk up beside the graveyard and then bear left at the end along the cobbled road past the houses. This soon deteriorates into a rough track; at the point where it hairpins to the right you should turn left and cross the stile by the green gate. Skirt the wood and bear right at the fork, following the track across the moorland. Enter the wood ahead and, some way on, bear right at the low footpath signpost, almost immediately crossing the head of a small waterfall. Walk on through the woods, leaving them by a stile and walk across the pasture. At the far end carefully cross the decrepit footbridge and walk up to the minor road.

Join this road and turn left, remaining with it to the end of the woods and there turning right, following the track you join up past the woods and out onto the open moor. Stick to the track, crossing through gates as necessary, until you reach the old, lonely signpost, its legend too weather-beaten to read. It points to the right, you want to turn left and follow the obvious path across the boggy moor, heading directly for the Winter Hill transmitter. From here there is an extensive view to the left across the Greater Manchester basin to the Peak District beyond. Cross a stile and aim for the small enclosure of conifers; keep these on your left and follow the line of the wall on your right. Cross the sunken driveway behind Higher Whittaker Farm and then head half-left across the field, aiming for the corner of the copse near which a stile gives access to a minor road. Turn right along this road and walk along over the dam of Belmont Reservoir. At the far end follow the path up to the left, join the main road and walk down into the village of Belmont to reach the Black Dog about 500 yards away.

4. The West Pennines: Wheelton

Route: Wheelton – Leeds & Liverpool Canal – Withnell Fold – Brinscall – Wheelton Plantation

Distance: 7 miles

Map: Explorer 287 West Pennine Moors

Start: The Dressers Arms, Wheelton

Access: The village of Wheelton is off the A674 Chorley to Blackburn road about three miles north-east of Chorley and two miles north-east of Junction 8 on the M61. To reach The Dressers Arms, which is at the east end of the village, drive past the Red Cat pub/restaurant and remain on the A674 as it bypasses the village to the south, then take the minor road which branches to the right and is signposted to Brinscall. The Dressers is on your left just a few yards up along this road.

The Dressers Arms (01254 830041)

There has been a pub here since well before the time of Oliver Cromwell. The "Inn on Friars Brow" was named to reflect the brothers of a friary that once stood at the top of the lane, since corrupted to "Briars Brow." Cromwell's persecution of Catholics in the area included these Brothers, nothing now remains of their former home. The pub's current name celebrates the craft of the stone dresser, the skilled workers who once laboured in the now-defunct quarry a few hundred yards from the pub. Old photographs of these craftsmen are a strong feature of the decor of the pub, its low beamed ceilings complementing the solid stone structure and massive fireplaces.

Until the late 1950s, the pub was the smallest in Lancashire, just a small stillage, serving hatch and drinking room. Extensions into neighbouring cottages, once the homes of the quarry foremen, saw this claim to fame extinguished, the "new" pub now having a separate games room, lounge and snug all within easy reach of the popular bar. Reasons for this popularity include Boddingtons Bitter and their own-brewed Wheelton Brewery beer as well as Timothy Taylor's Landlord and Stella lager on draught and variety of guest beers.

The Dressers Arms, Wheelton

Also on offer is an extensive range of bar snacks including such delights as Lamb Henry, liver and onions, large steak puddings and 18oz battered cod.

Landlords Steve and Trudie Turner welcome children and often host groups of ramblers; in the wettest of weather please wear boot protectors (e.g. plastic bags) or leave your boots in the porch. Opening hours are Mon-Sat, 11am – 11pm; Sun, noon – 10.30pm; bar meals are available from noon – 9.00pm every day. Sunday evenings has seen the meeting of the Old Wheelton Folk Club for the past 35 years. The pub has recently been extended and the restaurant leased to Cantonese Mrs Wans.

Withnell Fold

This hamlet owes its existence entirely to the Parke family who made a fortune from the cotton industry in nearby Preston. Diversifying from this industry, in 1843 the Parkes opened a paper mill on the bank of the canal at Withnell Fold Farm. To house the workers a "model" village was built, the benevolent Parkes also provided a reading room, shop, chapel and other communal facilities. The village survives intact although the mill, latterly used to produce bank-note paper, closed nearly 35 years ago; part of it was demolished and part taken over by small engineering and electrical firms which still thrive there. In recent years new housing has been added to the old core of the village and "executive" homes, many converted from old mill outbuildings and the reading room, overlook the canal. The village stocks remain in place on one side of the village square, a few yards away the old village farm is still in business.

Leeds & Liverpool Canal

One of England's major waterways, this cross-Pennine route took 43 years to complete from its inception in 1773 to the final link in 1817, delays being due both to financial problems and the Napoleonic wars. Some of the greatest feats of canal engineering help take the canal between the two great northern cities which it links – the mile long Burnley Embankment, the Bingley five-rise locks and the near-mile long Foulridge tunnel for example. The stretch of canal followed on this walk is perhaps the most scenic along its 127 mile length, contouring the hillside high above a meandering stream, well wooded and with distant views of the Pennine hills. It is very busy during the summer months with pleasure craft, less so in winter when it is rich with wildlife.

The Walk

From the Dressers walk down to the main road and cross straight over, heading down Victoria Street. A short distance downhill take the footpath signposted to the right up Stable Lane and walk up to the end. As you get to the house at the top look to your right to find the gate into the field, turn left and walk up this field. At the far end, leave by the stile next to the gate and walk straight ahead up the rutted track. Enter the field at the end and stick to the left-hand boundary, working left and downhill through the copse of chestnut trees to the lane at the foot of the slope. The view from this stand of trees extends over the nearby canal and across the Lancashire Plain cut by low, wooded ridges; on the horizon, the large gasometer is a famous landmark at the coastal resort of Southport.

Turn right along the lane and then, immediately before reaching the red-brick bungalow, turn left down along the track, cross the canal bridge and turn left, following the canal north with the water on your right. A great variety of birds may be encountered in the next

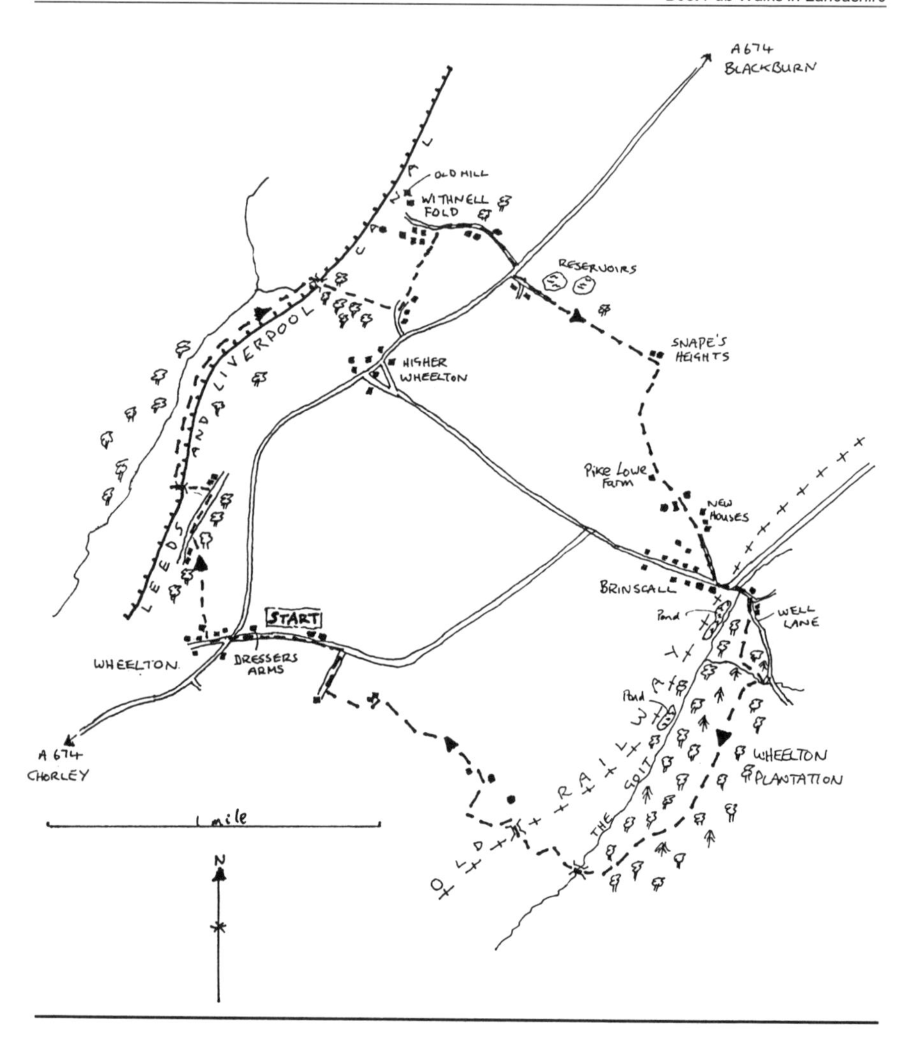

mile or so on the canal or down in the valley on the left. Watch out for kingfisher, coot, moorhen, little owl, sparrow hawk, kestrel, herons and jays to name but a few. You can see where the canal trough has undergone major repairs, a new concrete towpath on the near bank and tons of small limestone blocks on the far side to help prevent the wash created by boats eroding the steep wooded slope above.

Follow the towpath for about a mile. On your left a rusting mileage post records the distances to the terminal points of the canal whilst ahead the tall brick chimney at Withnell Fold peeks above the trees. Just before bridge 87 – the number is bolted to the bridge above the water – leave the towpath via the stile on the left, walk up to and cross the bridge and bear half-right along the path at the far end. Follow the path along the side of the valley, gradually rising up to the crest before reaching the massive aqueduct on your right. This is part of the complex system of pipelines developed to carry water from Thirlmere and other lakes in the Lake District to, initially, Manchester and more recently to other towns in mid and south Lancashire. Carry on along the crest of the valley aiming for the group of cottages in the middle distance, pausing for a moment to take in the view to the left which includes the fortified Hoghton Tower on the distant wooded crest of a hill, with the bulk of Longridge Fell forming the horizon.

The field narrows to a track before reaching the cottages. Cross the stile and bear left this side of the cottages. Follow the rough track through the gate and cross a field to reach the hamlet of Withnell Fold. Follow the track straight ahead until reaching the cobbled road. The route here is to the right but it's worth diverting left to walk down to the square and, beyond this, the old mill and the canal in this, one of the first planned industrial villages.

Walk up to the main road and cross straight over, walking a short way up Oakmere Avenue and then up the left fork. The road gradually deteriorates into a rough track passing housing to your right and two reservoirs to your left. Carry straight ahead up the track, which eventually fetches up at an isolated farm, Snape's Heights, near the hilltop. Walk ahead through the yard, cross the stile to the right of the gate and turn right, heading for the ruins of an old barn. From this point, the views to the north and west encompass Preston and the flat lands of the Fylde. Blackpool Tower is easily spotted whilst further to the north the concrete blocks mark Heysham nuclear power station. Clearer days will allow views to the southern peaks of the Lake District including Coniston Old Man, once Lancashire's highest point but since 1974 a part of Cumbria. Further to the east, the long back of Longridge Fell leads towards the Pennines and the distinctive shape of Pendle Hill before the horizon disappears behind the near hilltop.

Pass to the left of the old barn and walk along the rough roadway to Pike Lowe Farm, entering the yard by one stile and leaving by another at the far end. Continue along the track, walking to the left of the row of white-painted cottages to reach a new housing development. Here turn left and walk a short distance uphill, looking on your right for the tarmac footpath, which cuts down between two housing estates. Go along this – you'll know if you've found the correct path as there are some old stone barns a little way down on the right – and follow it all the way downhill, crossing a new access road en route. Continue down the road at the end to reach the old part of this, the village of Brinscall.

At the High Street turn left and walk to the bottom of the hill. Where the road bends sharp left continue straight on; to your right an old mill lodge now acts as the focal point of a large recreational area. Within a matter of yards turn right along Well Lane and look for the gate into the woodland on your right, just beside the derelict garage and rusting camper vans. Go through this gate and walk on into the woodlands.

Choice of route

This next section of the walk, whilst following a public right of way, involves a steep scramble at the head of a gorge. If you wish to avoid this then simply remain with Well Lane and wind uphill to the point where a fork occurs, the right-hand track being gated off. Cross the stile beside this gate to rejoin the walk.

Once in the woodland, Wheelton Plantation, follow the obvious path through the largely birch trees to reach a swift flowing stream. Turn left and work your way up alongside it, the route is not obvious, just take the line of least resistance through the trees and up the steepening gradient. In a short while you'll come to the foot of a waterfall tumbling over the lip of a long deserted quarry now festooned with mosses, ferns and trees, altogether a very picturesque spot. You need now to scramble to the top of the quarry. I found that the best route was well to the left of the waterfall, up a steep but distinct path beneath some tall fir trees. This brings you to a fence alongside the gate mentioned in the choice of route, above. Climb over the fence – I couldn't find a stile – and turn right to cross the bridge over the stream just above the waterfall, following the track round to the right and down into the woodlands.

Remain with this track all the way through the plantation, ignoring side paths off to the right. The birch are now largely supplanted by mature oak and beech woodland, dotted with sycamore and conifers. In season watch out – or listen – for jays and woodpeckers; some trees support enormous bracket fungi. At a number of sites, you will notice ruins and tumbled piles of dressed stone amongst the trees. These are the ruins of a calico print works and of the once locally important cottage industry of handloom weaving, largely extinct by the turn of the nineteenth century.

There's only one fork along the track, near to some of these ruins; keep right here. Some distance later, a track joins from the left. On leaving the woods cross the stile to your right (i.e. not the one leading onto the moorland) and walk across the bridge over The Goit, an artificial watercourse and part of the immense system of reservoirs and feeder channels in the Anglezarke area. Continue along the track ahead, eventually crossing the bridge over the old Chorley to Blackburn railway. Turn left along the road, then right having crossed the concrete bridge across a brook. Turn left immediately before the house and follow the track uphill to the right of the cottage on the hillside. At the end of the track cross the stile beside the gate and then follow the fence uphill, continuing straight up across the hillside by line of sight once the fence ends.

At the top left corner of the field, you'll reach the site of a drained pond. Some 50 yards to the right of this cross the rickety stile and follow the line of the fence in front of you. There are immense views to the left across Chorley and the Lancashire Plain to the Great Orme and the mountains of Snowdonia. Cross the stile ahead and walk to the wooden building in the farmyard graced with a notice "Danger, Sheep Dip." The way now is left, through the paddock and across the line of three stiles in quick succession, the first leading to a narrow footbridge, the others on either side of a driveway. Once over the third stile go half-left and then follow the holly hedge on your right round the corner and to the narrow end of the field. The stile here is partially blocked by a wire mesh fence and marked by an old stone gatepost. Cross this and walk ahead across the field, passing the wrecked vehicles to your left. On gaining the farm drive turn right and walk up to Briars Brow, turning left down the road to return to the Dressers Arms.

5. The West Pennines: Riley Green

Route: Riley Green – Darwen Gorge – Close Farm – Pleasington

Distance: 7 miles

Map: Explorer 287 West Pennine Moors

Start: The Royal Oak Hotel, Riley Green

Access: The hamlet of Riley Green is on the A675 Preston to Bolton road about six miles south-east of Preston and also off the A674 about three miles west of Blackburn. From Preston, take the A675 towards Bolton through Higher Walton and Hoghton. On reaching Riley Green, the pub is on the left just past the junction of the A675 with the A6061 beside which road the pub stands. From Blackburn take the A674 road towards Chorley and Preston and turn right along the A6061 at the sign to Preston, the pub is about a mile along on the right.

By rail, you can join the walk at Pleasington station, which is on the Preston to Blackburn/Colne line. There is a daily service, hourly Mondays to Saturdays, every two hours on Sundays.

The Royal Oak Hotel (01254 201445)

Until 1980 the Royal Oak was a part of the estate of nearby Hoghton Tower and had served estate workers since becoming a pub in 1711. Up to 1901 the driveway to the fortified manor house left the turnpike road beside the pub. It was originally a farm and the farmyard survived until the 1950s when the building was extended using estate elm wood; the room to your right as you face the bar was the farmyard. Since 1980 the pub has been supplied with mild and bitter by Daniel Thwaites of nearby Blackburn, kept in exemplary fashion by landlord Eric Hargreaves whose beer keeping skills have been recognised by the award of Membership of the British Institute of Innkeeping, a sought-after trade accolade.

It's a very popular pub both with locals, with travellers from nearby Blackburn, Preston and Chorley and boaters from the canal, and won the 'Pub of the Season in the North East Area' 2001. Apart from the beer one thing that appeals is the absence of any fruit machines, juke box or background music. The Royal Oak is well known to local rambling clubs who often use it as a base for their walks so as a reader of this book you're assured of a genuinely warm welcome.

Opening hours are Mon-Sat, 11.30am – 3.00pm and 5.30 – 11.00pm and Sun, noon – 10.30pm. Food from an extensive 'specials' board is served daily from noon – 2.00pm and 6.00 – 9.00pm – these meals can be taken in the bar or in the restaurant/dining room.

Hoghton Tower

Half a mile due north (i.e. behind) of the Royal Oak is the 16th-century fortified manor house of Hoghton Tower, home, since it was built, to the de Hoghton family. From many angles, the house is difficult to see, being built on a heavily wooded hilltop site; certainly from this walk you will see little more than tantalising glimpses of the building. It's worth going to see as a leading example of its genre, a footpath leads from beside the pub to the driveway leading up to the house, a half mile stroll across gently rising fields. Past visitors included King James I in 1617; so impressed was he by the repast provided for him by the de Hoghton family of the day that, as the well known story goes, he "Knighted" a loin of beef (presumably for services to the royal palate) since which time that particular cut of beef has been known as sirloin. The family fared rather less well, as the monarch's lengthy stay almost bankrupted them. The Tower is open to the public each Sunday from Easter to the end of October and also on Saturdays in July and August.

The Walk

Turn left from the Royal Oak and walk along the busy A6061 for about 200 yards to reach a farm drive on the left, marked by two cream painted gateposts and virtually opposite a red brick house. Go along this drive to the point where it hairpins to the left, at which point you should go through the gate-stile on your right (next to the field gate) and follow the sunken track down across the field, heading for the woods and the steep valley side. Cross a further stile, continue downhill to the end of the wire fence on your left and then carefully work your way down to the riverside. Walk downstream with this, the River Darwen, entering the wooded gorge via a stile. For the next half-mile or so simply follow this riverside path, crossing footbridges and side streams as necessary.

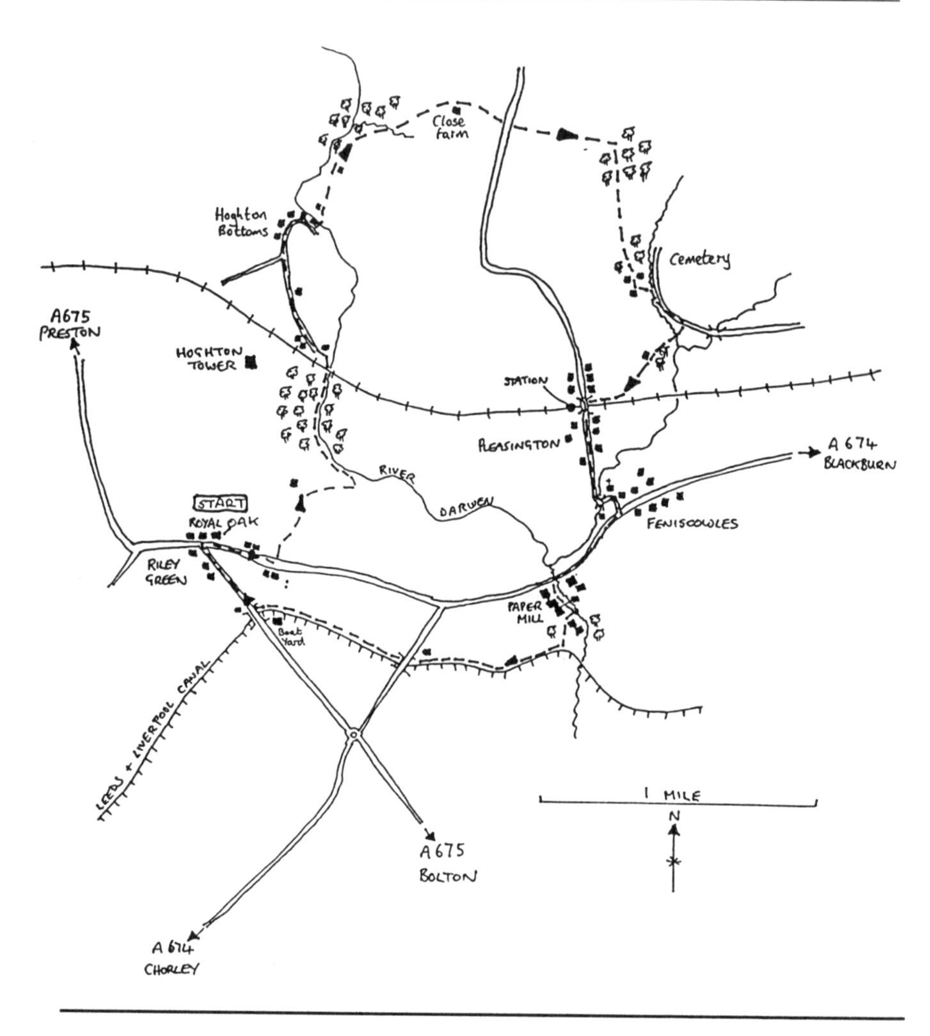

The gorge is rich in flora and fauna. In season great tracts of wild balsam, willowherb and butterbur blanket the banks of the Darwen. This river is cleaner than it at first may appear, evidenced by the occasional glimpse of a kingfisher and the large number of dipper, heron, ducks and coots, none of which species tolerate polluted water for long. At the weir the old mill leat splits off to the left, the footpath follows a wide track between this and the deepening gorge, particularly impressive when the river is in spate with a series of rapids, shoots and whirlpools. Pass beneath the viaduct carrying the

Preston to Blackburn/Colne railway over 100ft above the water and then follow the path away from the river, across a footbridge and past the site of one of the old mills which once provided employment for several hundred in the area; some cottages and the mill house remain standing.

Remain with the metalled road – Viaduct Road – you have now joined and at the end turn right to walk downhill into the hamlet of Hoghton Bottoms. Curve round right with the road and walk to the last cottage on the left. Immediately past this, turn left and cross the River Darwen on the green footbridge. From the bridge walk straight ahead, cross the low wooden stile and walk up past the stone barn and attached farmhouse. Wind round the end of this to cross a further stile, having crossed which, remain with the hedge to your left.

In a short while pass the scout hut to your right and then follow the track up around the hillside, leaving the river to carve its way through a second gorge. Looking back from this track, the chimneys of Hoghton Tower are visible standing above the trees. Remain with the woodland edge, crossing the first small brook and continuing the long, steady climb away from the river. At the top, and about 15 yards before the track crosses a second brook and bends sharply left, climb up to your right and look for the track ahead and to your left, easily identified by the sharp, red earth bank on its right. Walk along this track for a short way, entering the area of trees. The obvious gap in the line of trees to the left marks the point where a stream has been culverted. Cross here and walk straight up the grassy slope ahead of you to a stile in the wall on the ridge crest. Cross this and rest awhile to take in the extensive views to your left (north) which stretch over Preston and well up into the Forest of Bowland and to Kirkby Fell in the Yorkshire Dales. Your route lies straight ahead, aim for the stone farm building on the near horizon, Close Farm.

Leave the field by the stile to the left of the gate into the farmyard and walk through the small, rough pasture, leaving by the broken gate next to the old bathtub. At the subsequent gap in the wall turn right, bringing you to the entrance to Close Farm, marked by a cattle grid. Opposite you is a small stile at the point where the wire fence meets the thorn hedge; the legend "public footpath" is faintly painted on it in blue paint. Cross this and follow the line of the garden fence up the field. Where this turns right you turn half-right, pass through one of the gaps in the threadbare hedge and turn left, following the line of this hedge, then the next one. You will pass by a small circular walled enclosure en route, this is a small reservoir. At the far end of the second field, go through the gate, cross directly over the minor road and walk along the driveway opposite towards Maiden House Farm. From this point, you can pick out the Ribble estuary beyond Preston and distant views over the Fylde coast to the Lake District.

Where the drive bears right continue straight ahead and follow the line of hedge. Pass through the narrow stile by the gate and head straight across the field, leaving via the old gate by the holly tree. From here follow the line of trees across the next field, heading for the obvious wooden stile ahead of you, its position marked by a short section of plank fencing in the boundary hedge. Cross this stile and walk up the slight bank into the woods. After only a few yards join the main path and turn right in front of a silver birch tree, then walking gradually downhill. At the fork bear right and continue downhill, joining the line of a wall on your left. These woodlands are dotted with the well overgrown remains of small quarries, once worked for millstone grit building blocks.

At the end of the track, leave the woods via the steep stile and head straight down the large field, using the horizon-dominating transmitter that tops Winter Hill as a line of travel. Some way off to your left is Witton Park, a massive area of public parkland owned by Blackburn Borough Council. At the foot of the field (ignoring the remains of a hedge through which you have passed), you should walk down a sunken track that leads to the right of a small hangar of beech trees. Scramble up then to the path, which runs along the bank to the right of the track, now host to a stream. Climb the stile – the footings of which are cross-sections of a felled tree – and walk down to the surfaced road. Turn right along this, passing between new houses and an old barn, and walk along for about 50 yards. At the corner you should turn left in front of some red-brick houses. The actual footpath is immediately to this side of the gardens of these houses but is overgrown; local practice is to pass through the ruined metal gates and walk along the old driveway leading into the grounds of Pleasington Old Hall. After about 50 yards, follow the path off to the right along a line of tall fir trees to end up on a surfaced road serving the local cemetery. Turn right down this and walk down to and through the gates at the bottom.

Once through these gates bear right along the rough road running behind the sports field, crossing the stream to your right where it is culverted about 30 yards along. Virtually immediately, look forwards and to the right. You will see a footpath leading past an upright stile and into a narrow cleft. Before the stile, a track branches left and winds uphill, fir trees to its left, a wall to its right. This is the route you should follow, winding up the hillside to the old farm at the top. Cross the stile to enter the old yard of Tonguehill Farm, dating from 1735. Ahead, a footpath sign directs you left between two fallen barns. Cross the stile into the pasture here and follow the line of stiles virtually straight ahead, ending at a gate giving access to a narrow path that parallels the railway line. Walk along this path to its end and turn left along the road at the top. Pleasington station is down to your right whilst on the left is the Railway pub. Simply remain with the road, here called Victoria Road, for the next half mile, passing between late Victorian villas and earlier gritstone farm buildings. Wind across Walk Mill Bridge at the bottom (the mill burned down in 1864) and pass the picturesque, squat, Immanuel church, then walk steeply uphill to reach the busy A674 road.

Turn right and walk downhill. In the gorge to your right are the remains of several old mills, one mill house dating from 1830 survives. After about a third of a mile pass by the entrance to the Sun paper mill on your left and then cross the bridge over a deeply incised stream. Cross the road here and walk down the road into the paper mill complex. Walk along with the works on your right and the stream on your left until you come to the second security barrier (yes, it is a public right of way). Pass this second barrier (there's a security lodge on the left) and turn immediately right. You will know if you are in the right spot if the building on your right is painted blue and that on your left is built of prefabricated panelling. Walk up the hillside, joining the obvious footpath after 30 yards or so, and wind on up through the woods. At the top is the towpath of the Leeds & Liverpool Canal. Turn right along this, the water to your left. The justification for including this walk in the West Pennines is here, the canal acts as the border to the immense recreational area at this point. Remain with the towpath for a little over a mile to reach a boatyard on the opposite bank. Leave the towpath at the bridge here, turn right and walk up along the road back to the Royal Oak, a few yards to the right from the junction at the end.

6. The Forest of Bowland: Chipping

Route: Chipping – Knot Hill – Greystoneley – Dinkling Green – Birchen Lee

Distance: 9 miles

Map: Explorer OL41, Forest of Bowland & Ribblesdale

Start: The Sun Inn, Chipping

Access: Chipping is about 5 miles north of Longridge at the centre of a complex web of unclassified minor roads. It is, however, well signposted from Longridge which is, itself, about 7 miles north east of Preston along the B6243. Park in the free car park near the village centre.

The Sun Inn (01995 61206)

The inn stands in a commanding position right at the heart of Chipping at the junction of Windy Street and Talbot Street, looking down the steep slope of the latter over the village's two other pubs and post office to the old corn mill on Chipping Brook. Even this lofty perch was not enough for the builders in 1758 – the front door is only accessible up a considerable flight of stone steps. It's well worth the climb, however (and for exhausted ramblers the back door is step-less), as the Sun is everything you'd expect of a village local. Many a local has been gutted and changed beyond all recognition during the last two decades or so but thankfully, in the case of The Sun, little more than cosmetic surgery has been applied. The tiny old central bar remains intact, a serving hatch supplies the entrance passageway and games room whilst the main bar serves the locals snug. A room creates a comfortable extension to this snug (it was the kitchen) whilst a fourth room abuts the games room and passageway.

The whole pub has a traditional old-world charm, and landlord Steve Wadsworth serves a mix of popular guest cask ales as well as Boddingtons. Opening hours are Mon-Sat, noon – 11.00pm and Sun, noon – 10.30pm. Food is available daily at lunchtimes only: Mon-Fri, noon – 2.00pm and Sat-Sun, noon – 4.00pm, with a range of specials and full meals.

The pub started life as a farm; the range of outbuildings behind the pub remain from those days. When it became a pub, no one is quite sure. It was certainly one in 1835, however. In that year 19-year-old Elizabeth Dean was due to be married on November 5th. Taking a "stiffener" in The Sun before the ceremony she happened to glance across the road to the neighbouring church only to see her betrothed entering the churchyard to marry another. The distraught Elizabeth took herself to the pub's attic and hanged herself. Her simple gravestone stands next to the old yew in the churchyard.

The ghost of Elizabeth is said to haunt the pub, and has been seen by the landlord. Indeed the pub has an 'Officially Haunted' certificate from the National Ghost Federation who have stayed in the pub to witness the apparition.

The Forest of Bowland

Bowland is one of the few remaining wilderness areas in England, a high swathe of the western edge of the Pennines characterised by immense tracts of moorland deeply dissected by gorge-like cloughs, well wooded in their lower sections where the becks and rivers spill out into more gentle but equally inspiring rolling countryside. The whole area was designated an Area of Outstanding Natural Beauty (AONB) in 1964, one step away from a National Park. Golden Eagles have been seen in the area.

Virtually no roads penetrate the fastness of the high moors and fells. The only through road is a narrow, winding minor road that follows the chasm of a tributary of the River Hodder known widely as the Trough of Bowland; other roads or tracks peter out at isolated farmsteads or the gaunt ruins of shepherds' huts or old shooting lodges. Even footpaths and bridleways have only the most tenuous of holds in the area, these are essentially just a few old salters' ways or packhorse trails. One reason for this is that the area escaped virtually scot-free the attentions of even the most doughty Victorian quarrymen or water engineers. Thus whilst most areas of the Pennines are criss-crossed by tramway trackbeds, lead miners tracks, reservoir leats and quarry roads the sharp edges of the Bowland Fells acted as fortress walls and kept out the invaders.

Little can have changed since the Danes and Vikings, then the Normans, strove to turn the area to their advantage. It is the Normans we can thank for the name of the area. "Forest" refers not to a large, heavily wooded tract but to an area of exclusivity, a hunting area or Chase reserved for the use of the monarch or his earls and lords and subject to the often-barbaric Forest Law of the day in place of the common law. An early holder of the title to the Bowland area was John of Gaunt. The last truly wild deer was killed in about 1805, the deer you may see or hear today – Fallow, Roe, Sika or Muntjak are more recent introductions. This exclusivity largely remains even to this day. Large areas of Bowland are private shooting estates managed to ensure a good supply of grouse and to which access is jealously guarded, although some areas of the peripheral Fells are available to walkers under access agreements made between Lancashire County Council and the landowners, as is much of the North West Water land.

Chipping

The tight-knit village community can trace a history going back at least a thousand years. The word Chipping is derived from the Old English name for market, much more common in the West Country where towns famous for their wool markets – Chipping Campden, Chipping Norton – still prosper. This Chipping grew largely as a market to disperse the sheep and woollen products derived from the moorland pastures of the Forest of Bowland, immediately north of the village and sweeping down to the east and west; a sheep fair and sales is still held in September.

The parish church of St Bartholomew was established in the 10th century. Although much altered in Victorian times it retains its solid, squat tower, medieval font and stonework purported to be Saxon in origin; the old yew in the churchyard is said to be as old as the foundation. John Wesley preached at the church twice, the second time the parishioners rebelled against his interpretation of the scriptures and sent him packing; the incumbent rector, John Milner, travelled with him for a short time before returning to his sinecure at Chipping.

The village itself is largely of 17th- and 18th-century buildings with some more recent developments to the west and along Windy Lane on the site of an old brass foundry. There were once eight mills in the village producing goods as diverse as spindles and corn. Only one now survives as a working concern; the old Kirk Mill was once a cotton mill but now produces the chairs for which the village (and the manufacturers H.J. Berry) is famous. The walk passes this works tucked away in the deep clough of Chipping Brook north west of the church. Here also is the old village workhouse, now a row of cottages. The village school and almshouses date from the 1600s and result from the benevolence of a local mill owner, John Brabin, who made his fortune from local wool; these buildings are in Windy Street. Chipping remains a thriving local centre catering for the local agricultural community, the needs of the chair works, a growing number of tourists and as a commuting settlement for Preston. All this and virtually unspoilt to-boot, a combination to savour.

The Walk

(Several shallow fords and streams need to be crossed on this walk)

Walk down Talbot Street from the Sun, passing the other two village pubs (The Talbot and the Tillotsons Arms, both of which sell traditional ales) and cross Chipping Brook – look to your right to see the old corn mill and wheel, now a restaurant. Turn left at the war memorial along the road signposted for Dunsop Bridge and Bowland with Leagram and remain with it for about half a mile, passing an old estate lodge on your left. At the next turn to your left, which is the drive up to Leagram Hall, cross the cattle grid and wind up the drive through the parkland. When the woodland plantation is joined on your left continue up the drive to a point about half way up the woodland and then look to your right, just before reaching the oak tree nearest to the road on your right. Across the field beyond this (and slightly to the right) is a small plantation, uphill from which is an isolated oak. Leave the drive here and walk across the parkland to pass to the left of this isolated tree.

Once past the tree you will come to a stile over the wire fence. Cross this and then walk ahead, keeping the fence and/or hedge on your left. Views to your right take in the end of Longridge Fell and, further away, the distinctive shape of Pendle Hill, to your left are the high fells of Bowland. Remain with the fence/hedge and cross two stiles and a brook. You then need to ford or jump across the mill leat leading to Leagram Mill, then cross a rickety footbridge over Leagram Brook. Once across turn half-left and walk uphill out of the

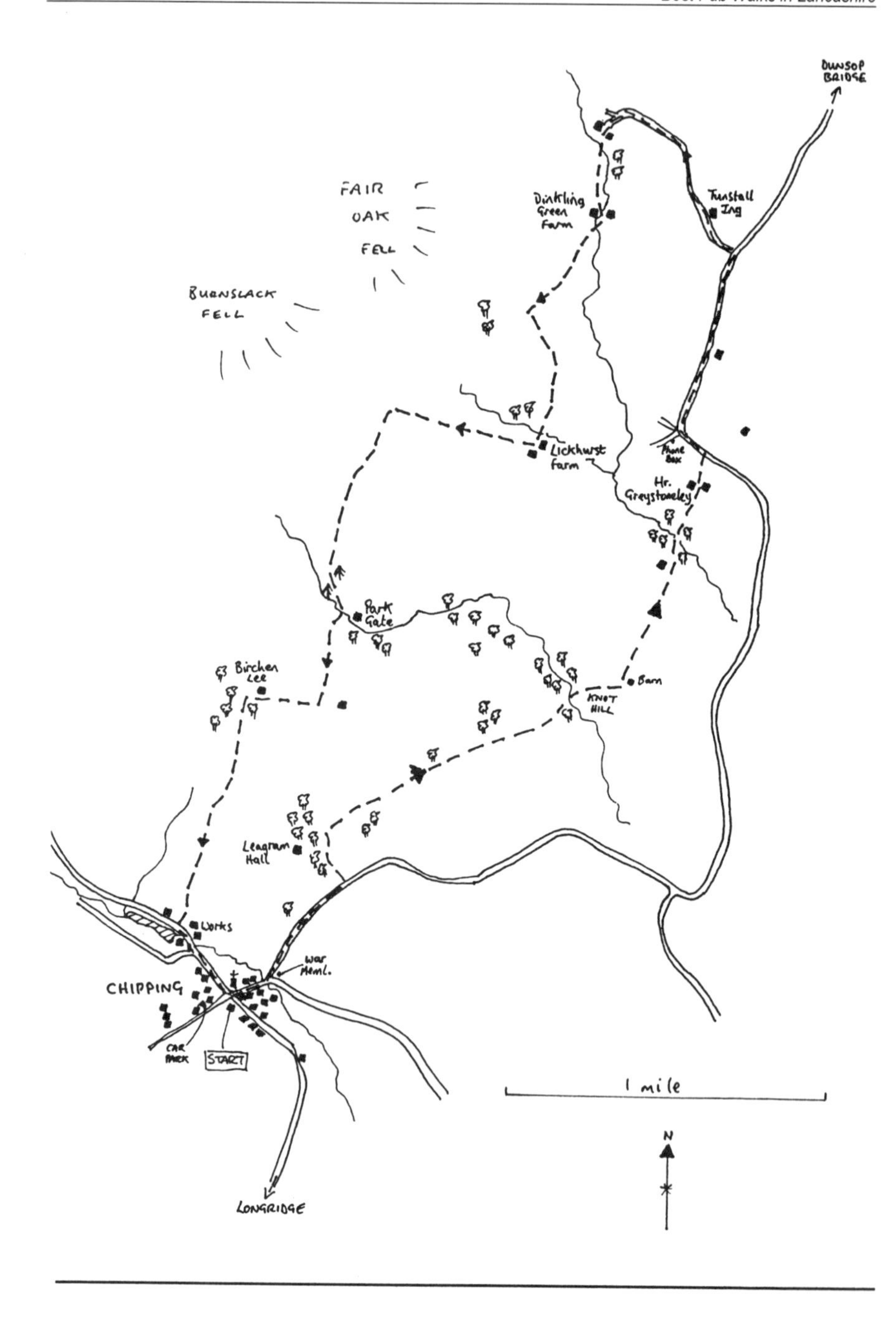

DUNSOP BRIDGE
FAIR OAK FELL
BURNSLACK FELL
Dinkling Green Farm
Tunstall Ing
Lickhurst Farm
Phone Box
Hr. Greystoneley
Park Gate
Birchen Lee
Barn
KNOT HILL
Leagram Hall
Works
War Meml.
CHIPPING
CAR PARK
START
LONGRIDGE
1 mile
N

Knot Hill and Fair Oak Fell

trees. Cross the stiles at the top and then walk across the field aiming for the left-hand side of the knoll ahead, Knot Hill. Simply walk around this limestone knoll which has been partially quarried away on its northern side; the workings are well overgrown. Look on your right for the semi-circular entrance to an old limekiln; this is where much of the quarried limestone will have ended up being roasted to provide lime for use to break down clayey soils or to be used as a base for whitewash.

Walk around to join the farm drive by the isolated Knot Barn and turn left along it, walking along to Lower Greystoneley, recently re-built, and through the farmyard. Go through the gate at the far end and walk downhill along the deteriorating track into the woods. At the ford look to the left to find a footbridge over Greystoneley Brook and then rejoin the track and walk up the far bank. Pass through the gate at the top and walk along to the farmhouse at Upper Greystoneley, passing between this on your left and the barns on your right. Remain with the driveway to reach a minor road and turn left along this, following it for the next mile or so, bearing sharp right after a short distance at the corner near the telephone box at the sign to Dunsop Bridge.

Moorland track above Lickhurst Farm

Walk up the hill through the knolly limestone area, pass beneath the line of electricity cables and about 150 yards later turn left along the minor road to Tunstall Ing; there's also a no through road sign and a cattle grid here. Walk on past the cottage and up around the end of the hillocks known as Long Knots; off to your right are extensive views over the beautiful Hodder Valley and up towards Gisburn Forest and the high moors and dales of North Yorkshire. The graceful bridge across the Hodder is Burholme Bridge. Where the road forks, keep left and walk down to the farm. Go through the gate into the yard and bear right, passing in front of the farmhouse and walking down the yard to the gate beside the bull pen. Go through this gate, down the track and across the footbridge beside the ford. Walk up the valley side opposite to a point just beyond the poultry houses but before the fence and turn left, walking along with the rail fence on your right. After 100 yards or so look for the steep stile on the right across the fence just where a gap in the line of trees appears. Cross this and aim for Dinkling Green Farm in the distance, crossing a further stile en route about 25 yards to the right of the gate in the fence.

Aim to enter the farmyard between the house on your right and the barn on the left, walking down a short ginnel to the farmyard. Continue through the yard to the black gate on the right between two buildings, going through this and down the lane beyond. Walk through the long, shallow ford and carry on up the rough track beyond, remaining with it for about 150 yards. Bear left at your end of the narrow band of woodland, pass through the gate at the end and follow the line of fence on your right. This is a good area to watch buzzard in action, sweeping effortlessly on their enormous wings across the lower slopes of Burnslack and Fair Oak Fells, their occasional plaintive "mewing" call breaking the still air of a summers day.

Go through the gate at the bottom and up the slope beyond, keeping the stream on your left to reach the gate on the corner at the top. Pass through this and walk along the edge of this field to the stone gateposts, go through these and head slightly right to the gate in the wall ahead. From here simply walk straight ahead and down into the deep, narrow valley ahead, aiming for the farm on the far side. Cross the stile to the left of the boggy area and walk down to the stream, walk over the footbridge and up the drive to Lickhurst Farm.

Bear right just before the buildings and go along the edge of the yard, following the track for about 30 yards and pass through the gate straight ahead of you, joining a rutted track leading towards the fells (if you get to the gate beside the poultry house you've gone just too far). Amble along this track, an old quarry road, for about half a mile to the point where it curves left and splits. Take the track virtually straight ahead – the one that passes through a shallow cutting – and once through the cutting angle gradually left away from the track and up onto the moor, aiming to walk just below the right-hand side of the summit of the hill on your left. Once here look for the tall Scots Pines and walk down to these. Far beyond you can see Longridge church spire and, beyond this, Preston.

You'll reach the nearest of these pine trees at the corner of two walls. Your route here is through the rickety gate and down past the fallen tree to the stream at the bottom. You will need to ford this then walk up the other bank to join the farm driveway from Park Gate Farm. Walk up the drive away from the farm and remain with it until the junction with a concreted drive nearly half a mile on. At this point, marked by an old milk churn stand, turn right and walk along to Birchen Lee Farm. Walk on past the farmhouse and through the small yard, turning left through the gate immediately through the yard and before you reach the stream. Follow the fence on the left, cross the brook at the end and then aim for the trees in the corner of the field ahead of you, in line with Longridge church spire. Cross the stile at this point, pass by the small overgrown quarry workings to your right and join the obvious track that comes up out of the deep valley of Dobson's Brook.

Follow this track left, heading towards Chipping, which is now visible some distance ahead. Climb the stile and remain to the right of the ditch and fence, walking gradually downhill to the millpond. Cross the stile a few yards up the driveway of the big house on the right and walk left down the drive to the minor road, turning left along this. The millpond is that which fed the Kirk Cotton Mill, now a chair works. The road winds through the works and past the old three-storey workhouse; bear left at the top to return to the village centre.

7. The Forest of Bowland: Whitewell

Route: Whitewell – Crimpton – Browsholme – Middle Lees

Distance: 6 miles

Map: Explorer OL41, Forest of Bowland & Ribblesdale

Start: The Inn at Whitewell

Access: The easiest way to find Whitewell is to start from Whalley, just south of Clitheroe and off the A59. Whitewell is signposted from Whalley, turn left along Station Road towards Mitton and then simply follow the signs for Whitewell and the Trough of Bowland through the maze of back roads for about eight miles.

The Inn at Whitewell (01200 448222)

Whitewell is The Inn. A handful of cottages, a chapel and a farm about half a mile to the north are all that keep this idyllic rural retreat company. Perched above a bend of the River Hodder this venerable inn – parts of which are over 500 years old – commands the ages-old route along the valley at a point where the river plunges headlong from a wide fertile plain into a deep, winding, wooded gorge, guarded at this northern end by the wooded dome of New Laund Hill. Nestling by the hotel, the tiny Georgian St Michael's church was completely rebuilt in 1817.

Eulogies about the hotel, of which the inn is an integral part, can be found in virtually every hotel guide, touring guide or pub guide, be it in English, American, German or Japanese. I won't deign to add to these; suffice to say that the hotel is virtually peerless for food and for the range of wines – over 140 – on offer and the world beats a path to its door. Perhaps surprisingly, this does not mean that the inn is terminally crowded or expensive. Quite the contrary, in fact, the pub itself is a modest and convivial establishment catering for a wide variety of users from the "Huntin', Shootin' and Fishin'" fraternity – the Hotel has a six mile stretch of the river's salmon and trout

The Inn at Whitewell

rights and entertains shooting parties at local farms – to ramblers and local farmers and has a brisk passing trade.

This mixed bag of clientele are entertained in "The Gallery" if you go by the evidence of the frosted glass in the front door which draws you into the cosy bar area. Heavily-leaded stone-mullioned windows help light the main room that has a welcoming open log fire as its centre-piece and is simply furnished with a pot-pourri of oak chairs, tables and settles on a carpeted flagstone floor. Old prints decorate the walls, which also sport the obligatory stuffed fox heads and a case of stuffed owls and birds of prey. The inn is stocked by 'Interbrew' and has occasional guest beers such as Marston's Pedigree. Adjoining the main room is a lounge area with another roaring fire, a baby grand piano, long case clock, settles and a small library of local interest books.

Proprietor Richard Bowman offers a very varied bar meals menu which includes such gems as Bangers and Champ and Fisherman's Pie. Meals are available from noon – 2.00pm and 7.30 – 9.30pm, the inn itself is open between 11am – 3pm and 6pm – 11pm and children are welcome.

The Walk

Start up the narrow road opposite the hotel, bear left and in a few yards look on the right for a flight of steps climbing up to a gate. Pass through this gate and walk up the field aiming for the lone cottage ahead with the cream painted side wall, Seed Hill. The actual right of way is to turn left and walk behind the cottage, then following the line of bushes and trees uphill and on your right although the evidence is that many walkers walk up in front of the cottage to join this old hedgerow. Once at the top of the field go through the gate and angle slightly to the left, aiming for the obvious gate in the wall to the left of the limestone knoll at the top end of this field. On your right beside this gate is the rounded mouth of an old limekiln where rock quarried from the knoll was roasted. Look carefully at the blocks of stone which make up the dry stone wall by the gate, they're full of fossils, largely crinoids, a now-extinct kind of long stemmed sea-lily distantly related to starfish. Behind you are extensive views across the Hodder valley to Mellor Knoll and Totridge Fell, at over 1600ft one of Bowland's highest points.

Cross straight over the narrow road here and go through the gate opposite. Bear right and walk along the track for a short while, leaving it before it bends left to find the ladder stile over the wall ahead. Once over this walk up to the isolated group of trees in the pasture ahead. These are growing round a series of potholes and natural sinks in the porous limestone at this spot. Pass to the left of these trees and then bear slightly right and walk ahead across the rough pasture, up to the right of the shallow valley. On reaching the wall at the far end look for the narrow but obvious gap through the thick plantation of conifers on the other side of this wall, it is about 100 yards up from the corner; the way over the wall is a rough stone step stile opposite this gap. Walk through the woods and, on emerging from such, go over the stile on the left and then head across the field to the line of trees at the far side. Pass through this line via the two gates and walk on to the farm, Crimpton, following the waymark arrows through the farmyard and walking on to the minor road at the end of the drive.

Turn right at the end and take a few paces uphill, looking on your left for the small stile beside the stump of an old telegraph pole. Climb this stile and then walk to your right, uphill along the obvious

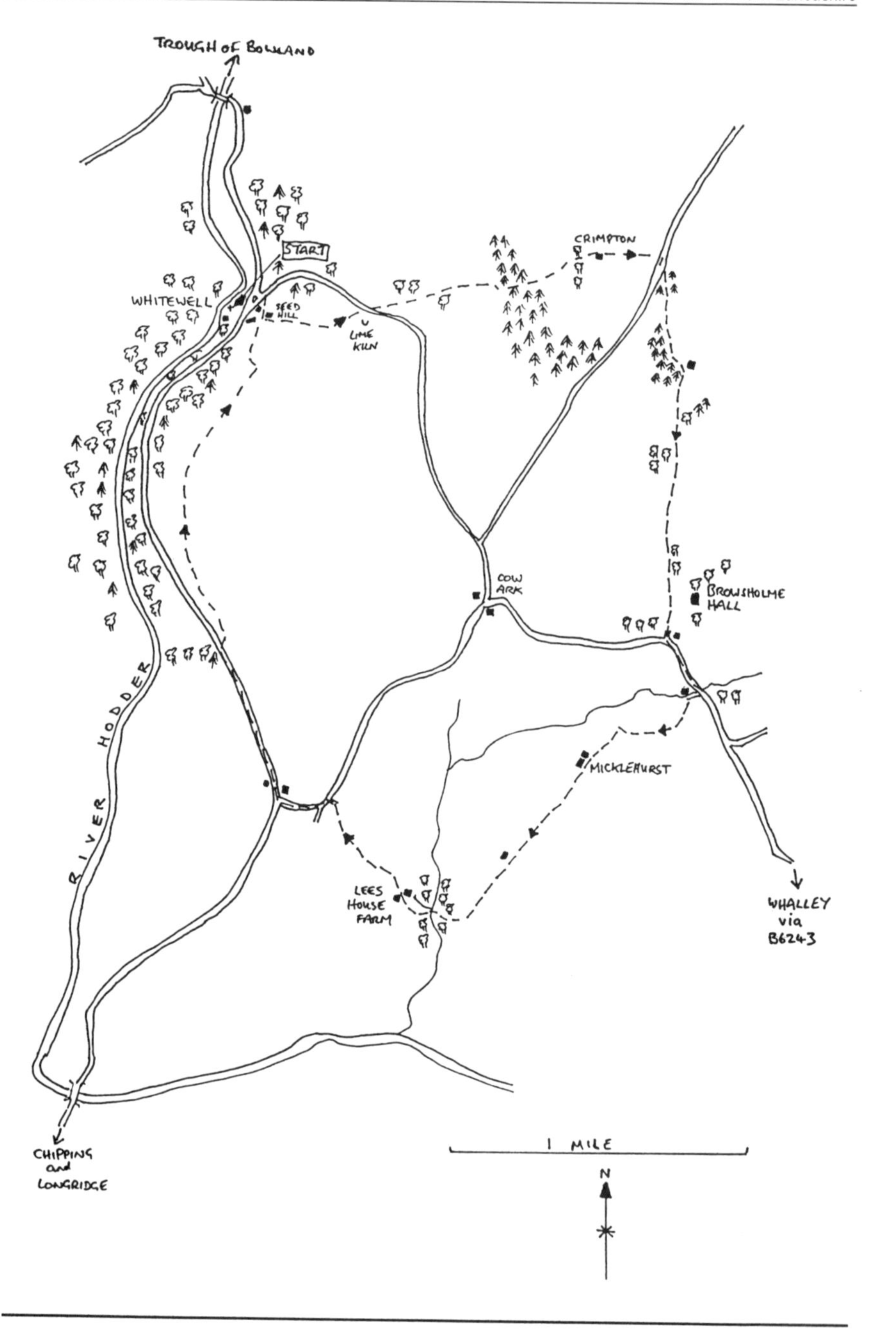
TROUGH OF BOWLAND
START
WHITEWELL
SEED HILL
LIME KILN
CRIMPTON
COW ARK
BROWSHOLME HALL
RIVER HODDER
MICKLEHURST
LEES HOUSE FARM
WHALLEY via B6243
CHIPPING and LONGRIDGE
1 MILE
N

line up through the conifers. At the top of the plantation cross the stile and turn left to follow the fence to the corner of the trees. From here, walk up the field heading for the chimneys that poke just above the ridge top. Cross the track at the top and walk to the corner of the woodland near the cottage, going over the stile here (formed by two piles of stones concreted together) and then following the woodland edge. The cottage is dwarfed by a peculiar folly of a structure, reminiscent of a massive Tudor chimney stack but evidently not functioning as such.

Turn right at the corner of the trees, cross another stone-pile stile and walk away from the cottage to the isolated brick shed. Turn your back on the woodland edge here and walk half-right across the large field, aiming for the right-hand edge of the loose area of beech trees which are, themselves, to the right of a conifer plantation; just head for the point where the line of telegraph poles leaves the field. At the far corner of the beeches, cross the stile beside the gate and turn right, walking to the far end of the pond on your left. From here, walk down across the pasture to the left corner of the isolated spinney of fir and deciduous trees. Go down the track beside these trees and then look to the bottom end of the subsequent field to sight the track winding away from a series of gates. Walk down to this, cross the cattle grid and walk along this track to its end. Off in the trees to the left is Browsholme (pronounced brewzum) Hall, ancestral home of the Parker family and open to the public at various times of the year. At the bottom of the track go through the gate and walk on to the minor road at the sharp corner beside the lodge house. Bear left along the road and walk downhill to cross Mill Brook.

Immediately you've crossed the bridge, go through the gate on your right, climb the steep bank up to the field and walk across it to the gate and stile in the fence opposite. The ridge dominating the horizon is Longridge Fell; behind you fleeting glimpses of Browsholme Hall in the woodlands. Turn right along the drive here and follow it round to Micklehurst Farm. Walk through the yard in front of the house, leaving by the gate at the far end and walk to the end of the pasture. Cross through the gate beside the stunted thorn tree here and join the track on your right, which leads to the isolated Kinder Barn. Pass to the left of the barn and walk down the long field beyond, keeping to its right-hand boundary. At the end go through the gate, turn right and go through the neighbouring gate into the steeply sloping pasture. Walk diagonally down the pasture, aiming to pass to the left of the large oak tree at the edge of the wooded valley bottom.

Work down the valley side to the stream and walk upstream to find and cross the solid wooden footbridge. Such stalwart effort at providing this bridge is largely wasted by the complete lack of any waymarking or obvious path at the far side. You need to work up the steep wooded slope beyond, favouring your right hand and roughly following the line of the deep cleft off to the right – it really is a matter of following the line of least resistance. At the top of the bank you will find yourself at Lees House Farm. The footpath here joins the driveway of the farm. Walk to your right through the farmyard and wind round with this driveway to the road at the end. Turn left and then sharp right with the surfaced road; the long straight trackway leaving at this sharp corner is the line of a Roman road from Ribchester. When you reach the junction turn right, following the sign for Whitewell, and remain with this road for about half a mile.

When you reach the arm of woodland on your left, go through the substantial black-painted metal gate on your right opposite the far corner of this woodland. Bear left and walk along the field virtually parallel with the road, aiming to go through the tall metal kissing gate beside the massive metal gate in the wall at the far end. Once through this walk ahead immediately below the small old quarry working and then follow the line of the wire fence around the contour, crossing stiles as and when necessary to reach a second tall kissing gate. Pass through this and look up to the right to the old quarry working which has exposed a nicely folded area of banded limestone. Walk on for a few yards to the field gate on the left. Go through this and then follow the old track beyond, winding round the hillside and slowly loosing height. The wisps of smoke curling up out of the valley ahead emanate from the inn's chimneys; beyond this is an excellent view up the Hodder to the graceful Burholme Bridge. Walk down to the side of Seed Hill Cottage and then retrace the initial part of the walk to reach the inn.

8. The Forest of Bowland: Slaidburn

Route: Slaidburn – Burn House – Beatrix – Newton

Distance: 7 miles

Map: Explorer OL41, Forest of Bowland & Ribblesdale

Start: Hark to Bounty Inn, Slaidburn, Nr Clitheroe BB7 3EP

Access: Slaidburn is about nine miles to the north of Clitheroe on the B6478. From Clitheroe take the road to Waddington, thence climbing high over the moors to Newton where a right turn will bring you to Slaidburn about two miles further on. The Hark to Bounty Inn is in the centre of the village close to the war memorial. If you can't park at the pub then turn right at the sign to Settle and wind down to the car park near the river.

Hark to Bounty Inn (01200 446246)

Whilst justifiably proud of the excellent and unusual foods on offer (including home-made rabbit pie and lots of fish dishes), a glance ahead to the bar reveals that the fare offered by Isobel Bristow is certainly not at the expense of draught beers. You have a choice of Theakston's Best Bitter, Old Peculiar and Courage Directors all on handpump.

This is one of the most famous pubs in Lancashire, largely because of its unusual name. This dates back to 1875 when the local squire was heard to remark to his drinking companions during a break from the hunt, "Hark to Bounty," referring to the baying of his favourite foxhound which could be heard above the barking of its peers in the square outside. An unusual name although not unique, there are several "Hark to" pub names in the Bury area.

The pub itself dates back to the 13th century and for many years doubled as the local courthouse on the regular round of the travelling justices on the Lancaster to York circuit. An external staircase still gives access to the first floor courtroom, which was last used, for judicial purposes, in 1937. Nowadays the wood-panelled room is available for functions but can be viewed upon request. In the winter one of the great draws of the pub is the splendid fire in a large hearth surrounded by highly polished brass and copper, just a short step from the bar.

Opening hours are Mon-Sat 11.00am – 11.00pm, Sun noon – 10.30pm; the varied menu may be sampled in the winter months from 6.00pm – 8.00pm and from noon – 2.00pm and 6.00pm – 9.00pm in summer. If you're captivated by the pub and the area (and it's hard not to be) then you can also stay at the Hark to Bounty Inn.

Slaidburn

This is a gem of a village, little more than a cluster of cottages and farms huddled round a crossing of ways high up the Hodder valley. This crossroads has been there for aeons; some of the old salters' roads across Bowland homed in on the place that, in consequence, developed as the administrative centre for the Forest of Bowland, hence the courtroom above the pub. Visually, hardly anything has changed over the centuries, as if the village had been mothballed. Virtually the only new building is a modest little health centre tucked away off one of the village roads; other "new" buildings include a poorhouse by the green dating from 1852 and the nearby Methodist Chapel founded in 1821.

For the most part, however, the tiny sandstone cottages have looked at each other across the narrow streets and cobbled pavements for three or four hundred years. Some retain their solid external stairs and mounting blocks, harking back to the days when the upper storeys were used as haylofts and horses ruled the streets; the motor vehicle is an intruder here. Many of the storerooms and barns still remain in use amongst and alongside these cottages; no conversions or modernisations have been allowed, in all probability because much of the village belongs to one family with a great sense of tradition and propriety. One notable conversion has occurred, however; The Old Black Bull pub is now a youth hostel. Apart from upland farming – the name Slaidburn means "sheep field overlooking a river" – the villagers used to make a living from rearing rabbits and processing their pelts for use in the fur trade, or from working galena (lead) veins in the surrounding hills.

St Andrew's church, to the south of the village, is a 15th-century rebuild of a much older structure; the list of rectors goes back to 1246

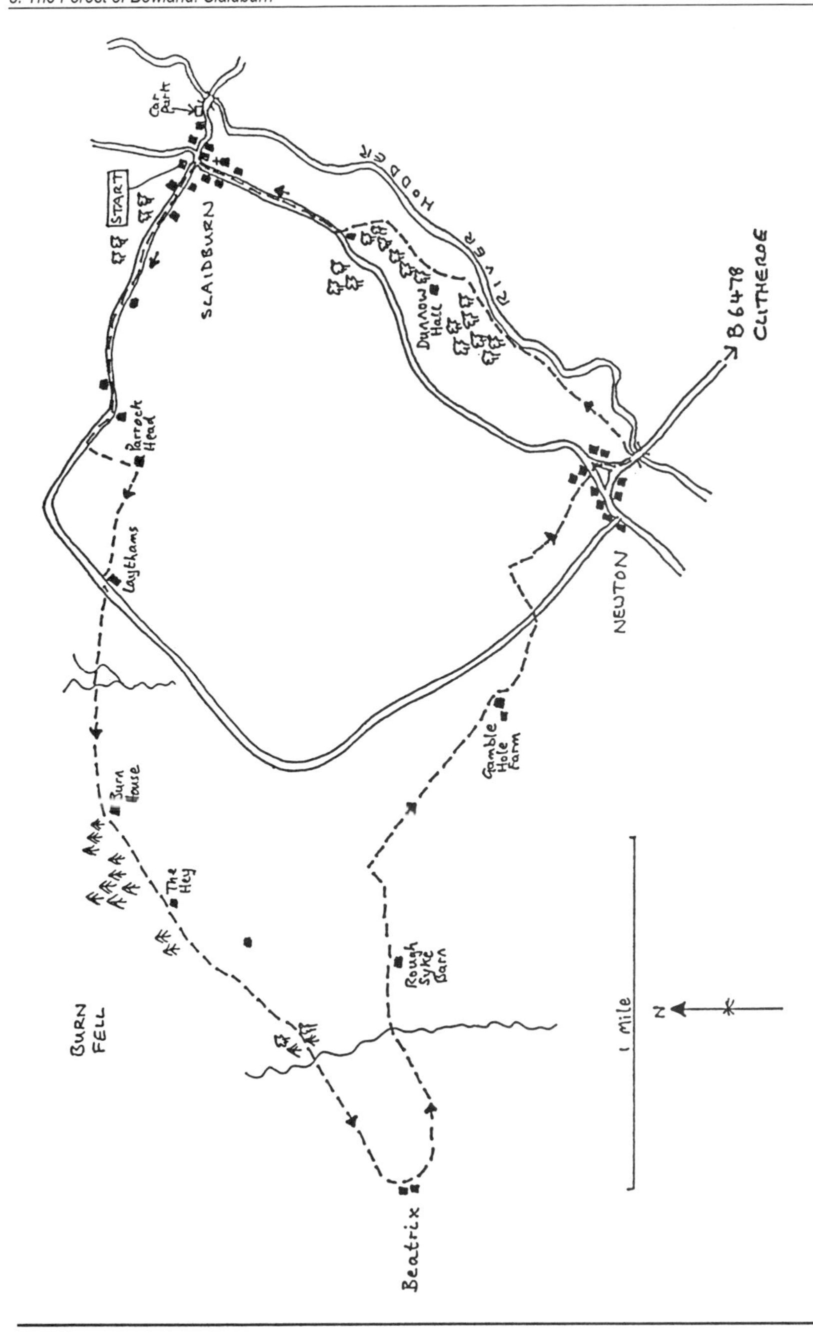
START
Car Park
SLAIDBURN
RIVER HODDER
Dunnow Hall
B6478
CLITHEROE
Parrock Head
Laythams
NEWTON
Gamble Hole Farm
Burn House
The Hey
Rough Syke Barn
BURN FELL
Beatrix
1 Mile
N

but a pre-Norman foundation is likely. Inside are some fine box pews dating back to the 1600s, retaining the names of the families by which they were installed and used, and an unusual three-tier pulpit. There is also a beautifully carved wooden chancel screen dated 1634. Next to the churchyard stands the village grammar school, endowed in 1717 and overflowing with tiny mullioned windows.

The Walk

Turn right out of the pub and walk down the hill, then wind gradually uphill out of the village. Down in the trees to the right are the remains of the old mill dam and leat, just upstream this Croasdale Beck winds through a tight wooded valley. Stay with this road for about a mile; it is very quiet as it doesn't lead to anywhere. Pass by Ellerbeck Hall, dating from 1694, on your left and walk up the hill beyond, turning left at the top along the driveway to Parrock Head Hotel and restaurant. Walk through the car park in front of this converted farmhouse, go through the gate at the end and turn right before you get to the barn. Pass through the field gate and walk to the wall along the right of the field. Climb the stile at the top end of the field and remain with the wall on your right to the point where it bends right; from here walk across the field to the long, low, white building, Laythams.

Go through the gate to the right of the house and turn left along the road, then go through the rusty field gate on the right, opposite the middle of Laythams. Head half-left across the field, aiming for the farm that is all but hidden in the left-hand fir plantation on the lower fell-side ahead. Cross the stile and walk to the corner of the fence ahead, walking along with this on your right for a short distance. Cross straight over the surfaced field track and a couple of brooks and walk across the rough pasture to the stile a few yards to the right of the short section of rail fencing. Climb this stile and walk to the wall on the left, walking uphill with this to the stone step stile protected by some wooden rail fence. Look at the stones in the wall beside this stile, some of them are limestone rich in fossils, mostly crinoids but also corals and shells. Once over this head across the field towards the fir trees just behind Burn House. Gain the roadway and follow it along behind the farm, then remaining with it for a good half mile, passing behind a further moorland edge house, The Hey.

The prospect from the road here is excellent. To your right the long line of Burn Fell, ahead a veritable family of fell tops above Dunsop Bridge culminating in Totridge Fell, one of the highest in the Forest of Bowland. Off to the left is limestone country; Rough Syke Beck in the valley below marks the approximate boundary between the gritstones and limestones in this part of Bowland, down the valley is the small, sharp knoll known locally as the Sugar Loaf. This varied landscape is home to a variety of birds of prey, you may see buzzard, hen harriers, peregrine falcon and little, short-eared and barn owls; listen out too for the distinct loud, laughing call of the green woodpecker.

Walk along the road from The Hey to the point where it kinks to pass through the line of the old thorn fence, a point marked by a single stone gatepost. Here, go through the field gate to the right and walk alongside the fence/ditch on your left to the end of the pasture. You now need to enter the area of woodland ahead, the easiest if not most convenient way is to climb the fence where the ditch passes beneath it. Walk ahead across the boggy patch and alongside the fence, making your way through the trees and downhill as best you can to the small gate through the fence at the bottom of the slope. Ford the stream beyond this and then scramble up the steep slope opposite, following the obvious but narrow path with a brook in a cleft to your right.

At the top of the slope keep the fence to your right and walk on across the moorland pastures, eventually ending up about half a mile later on a farm drive just beside Beatrix Farm. Turn left and walk through the farmyard with the house and barn to your right, at the far end following the left-hand track gently up the hillside. In about 100 yards, where this track passes between two thorn trees and into a field on your right, angle off to the left up the truncated track and then walk down to the barn which you'll soon be able to see. Pass to the left of the barn and head slightly left across the field to the obvious gate at the bottom. Continue to walk downhill, heading in line for the barn on the hillside opposite. Cross the stream in the area of gnarled old woodland in the valley bottom, climb the stile beyond and walk up the old track past Rough Syke Barn, then aiming for the gate you can see on the crest of the hill, ahead.

Climb the railway-sleeper stile to the left of this gate and walk on along the track beyond around to the left of the hilltop. On reaching the gate on your left pass through it and walk along the track, Bull Lane. At the point where this turns sharp right, pause to appreciate the view ahead that stretches across the Forest of Bowland to the Three Peaks area in the Yorkshire Dales; you should be able to make out Pen-y-Ghent and Ingleborough. Remain with the track for a few yards more until it turns sharp left, at which point go through the little wooden gate in the fence ahead, aiming then across the fields to the farm nestling beneath the trees in the distance. The fields are pock-marked with small hollows. These are natural features known as shake holes, a diagnostic feature of limestone terrain. Rainwater dissolves away locally-finely jointed limestone causing the land surface to sag, sometimes quite considerably where small caverns underlie the surface.

Pass through the gate to the left of the barn and walk down through the farmyard of Gamble Hole Farm. At the far end bear right immediately beyond the corrugated iron barns and follow the oak tree-lined track along the right-hand edge of the field. At the far end of the field leave the track to run ahead and go through the gate to the left, then walking to the diagonally opposite left-hand corner of the field you are now in. Go through the gate here and step down to the road. Cross straight over this and climb the stone step stile through the wall opposite just left of the thorn bush. Walk ahead across the field, cross the stream on the stone slab bridge and walk up through the narrow neck of the field ahead. Once through this neck bear right and walk down the narrow field towards the small barn. Leave this field near the corner to the right of the barn and continue away from the barn to the gate through the middle of the hedge ahead. At this point, the tiny village of Newton comes into view down below you. Walk to the bottom left-hand corner of the field you're now in, climb the stone stile into the work yard and walk down through this yard to the road at the bottom, right in the middle of Newton.

The village is little more than a cluster of old houses and cottages around a green; there is also an old Quaker meeting house. Walk down the road signposted to Clitheroe and pass by The Parkers Arms (Whitbread-based real ales) to reach the old two-arched bridge over the Hodder. Don't cross this but take the footpath on the left immediately before the bridge, walk upstream for a few yards and go through the little gate that gives access to a stone causeway alongside the water. At the end of this leave the river for a while and walk

Beatrix and Whin Fell, Slaidburn

ahead with the wall on your right. Cross the slab footbridge on your right, climb the stile and turn left, then walking along with the brook on your left. Walk towards the steep, wooded hillside ahead, go through the stile at the end and then follow the path through the woods at the foot of Great Dunnow hill. At the far end go through the kissing gate and walk ahead across the field, the mansion that is Dunnow Hall coming into view on your left. Turn left along the roughly surfaced track that cuts across the field and follow this around the foot of the woodlands away from the hall. When you reach the lodge house at the end, turn right along the road to return to Slaidburn.

9. South West Lancashire: Lydiate

Route: Lydiate – Walsh Hall – Clieves Hills – Bangor's Green – Downholland Cross

Distance: 8.5 miles

Map: Explorer 285, Southport & Chorley

Start: Scotch Piper Inn, Southport Road, Lydiate, Merseyside L31 4HD

Access: Lydiate village is immediately north of Maghull at the junction of the A59 and A567 roads about eight miles north of Liverpool City Centre and four miles south-west of Ormskirk. The Scotch Piper Inn is on the A567 Maghull to Southport road, about a mile north of the centre of Lydiate, and is on the left as you travel towards Southport.

Scotch Piper Inn (0151 526 0503)

Centuries ago, The Scotch Piper Inn was called The Royal Oak. The reason for this is apparent in one of the pub's three public rooms where part of a massive oak tree can still be seen; the pub was constructed around the tree that was used as a main support, a not uncommon practice in pre-Tudor days. The name Scotch Piper was adopted following the Jacobite uprising of 1745; retreating from Derby in disarray a band of Bonnie Prince Charlie's surviving troops took shelter in the pub and left one of their number, a piper, to be nursed back to health there, hidden from the avenging troops of George II.

Little can have changed since then or, indeed, since the remarkable tenancy of the Moorcroft family commenced in the middle of the 15th century. From then until 1945 the pub was owned and run by a member of the family. The thatched pub predates even them, however, dating from 1320 which makes it, as is proudly proclaimed on the front wall, the oldest pub in Lancashire. Some simple wooden benches complement massive beams, low ceilings and stone floors, upholstered seating and the occasional settle in the public rooms. Emulsioned walls contrast sharply with the dark beams and few paintings, photographs or artefacts decorate the walls, this very lack

The Scotch Piper, Lydiate

seems to add to the character of the place. In season, open fires blaze in the hearths of the bar area and the lounge, making for a very friendly, cosy atmosphere. Children are not allowed in the pub, but dogs are welcome. The licensees, Mrs Anne Marie and Fred Rigby, keep a very tasty pint of Burtonwood Bitter and Top Hat, and in the winter months a strong winter ale may be available. The Scotch Piper Inn is renowned for its excellent Guinness.

All in all, it's a great basic pub, recognised as such in 1986 when CAMRA awarded it the joint top award for pub preservation. Opening hours are noon – 3.00pm and 5.30pm – 11.00pm. Note – no food is served.

South West Lancashire and the Lancashire Plain

The very word "plain" strikes fear into the heart of many a walker, visions of unending tracts of the flat, virtually featureless countryside of parts of East Anglia or the Netherlands haunting their dreams. The Lancashire Plain is not like that. Certainly, this area of Lancashire is characterised by drainage ditches, hedgeless fields and rich farmland intensively used by market gardeners and to this extent it resembles Holland. Where it scores its advantages, however, are in the low, wooded ridges which cut into the area, the old villages that dot the plain and the ever-present views to the looming mass of the West Pennines and the Upholland Hills immediately to the east. These features combine to offer easy, pleasant walking through ever-changing farmland and gently undulating country-side.

The rich, black soil of the area is a result of inundation by the sea following the last great ice age some twelve thousand years ago; a combination of silts and sands makes this area one of the market gardens of England, famed for root crops, lettuce and brassicas. Until the 1960s trainloads of produce travelled overnight on special trains to the great London markets at Covent Garden and Nine Elms. The soils were made cultivable largely in the 18th and early-19th centuries by construction of drainage ditches; windmills once provided the wherewithal to pump the water into these ditches but they have now been replaced by electric pumps.

Before this, the area was largely low lying rough pasture and marsh, the famous Lancashire Mosslands. Powerful families such as the Asshetons and the Hesketh owned the land alongside a number of monastic foundations; income was generated from vaccaries (cattle farms) and from flax and hemp growing for the fledgling linen industry. Settlements grew up and villages developed on any available high ground – low sandy ridges and clayey knolls – as any sweeping view around the horizon will today testify; squat, sandstone church spires and towers seem to be everywhere in this once staunchly Catholic area.

The first stirrings of the Pennines mark the eastern edge of the plain and are a convenient boundary for South West Lancashire. The ridge of the Upholland Hills reaches only very modest heights at Harrock and Billinge Hills and bears no resemblance to the "Backbone of England" just a few miles beyond, being an extension of the New Red Sandstones more familiar in Cheshire rather than the older Millstone Grits of the high Pennines.

The Walk

Leave the pub and turn right, heading south along the road towards Lydiate village centre. On reaching the bridge over the canal cross the road and take the footpath at the far end of the bridge, signposted to Pygon's Hill Lane. This brings you down to the Leeds and Liverpool Canal on the opposite side to the towpath. Walk along, with the water on your left, for about a mile. Many of the pastures hereabouts are in use as paddocks for racehorses, there are also a rich variety of water birds on and around the canal which here is thickly lined with willow trees and more akin to a natural watercourse.

Just past the cottages is a semi-circular embayment in the canal bank. This is a winding hole (pronounced as in "Wind in the Willows"), used as a place to turn boats; all canals have one every few miles. On reaching the narrow road just past this leave the canal and turn right along the road. About 100 yards along on the right is a private drive leading to Jackson's Bridge Farm. Opposite this is a somewhat hidden public footpath sign to Back Lane. Take this path, sticking to the fence on your left. Cross the wide bridge over the drainage ditch and bear half-right. The path is fairly obvious – in line of sight it heads for the church steeple on the horizon – and leads diagonally across the field to two hazel trees, the tallest remaining in a threadbare hedge. This in itself is unusual, as you will see few hedges on this walk; field boundaries are marked largely by dykes, drainage ditches or farm tracks and are often rich in wild flowers.

Keeping the hazel trees, then the ditch, on your right walk for a few hundred yards north east towards the low ridge of the Clieves Hills. At this point, the right of way takes an illogical diversion. Ahead of you is a small clump of trees, to the right three sets of buildings. You should turn right when opposite the middle set and aim for the right of these cottages. On gaining the roadway here turn left and walk for about 100 yards. Ahead on your left is a white metal fence and about 20 yards before this are two wooden posts also on the left, these mark the footpath. There is a broken down footpath sign to "Birches Brow ½ mile" here at the time of writing. Head for the clump of willows and skirt these on the left, following the obvious track between the fields to reach Walsh Hall Farm. Many of the rather gnarled trees in this area display a distinctive pattern of growth on their eastward side making them seem to lean to the right. This is due to the effect of the prevailing south west wind that whips in across the plain from Liverpool Bay, half a dozen miles to the west, most branches growing on the sheltered leeward side of the trees. Pass between the barn on your right and the farmhouse off to your left, turn right along the driveway and walk along to the main road.

Turn left along the road and then almost immediately right up Clieves Hills Lane. Follow the gentle slope uphill past Firs Lane and then take the track off to the right about 20 yards before the cream-painted house on the left. The track rises past a cottage on your right, soon spilling into the fields, home to a large number of grey partridge. To the right (south) are extensive views across Liverpool; you can easily pick out the two cathedrals, one at each end of Hope Street, and the cranes at the docks. Beyond is the sandstone ridge that forms the spine of the Wirral Peninsular and, further away still, the mountains of both north-east Wales and Snowdonia. You can also pick out the massive limestone headland of the Great Orme at Llandudno, named after the same saint as the town of Ormskirk.

Aim to leave the fields to the left of the two modern houses and go straight across the road into Small Lane, bearing right at the end into Gaw Hill Lane. Remain with this, named after the highest point in the Clieves Hills at 266ft, and climb gently up onto the ridge of the hills. Turn left along Holly Lane and walk northwards just below the ridge top. Views to the west stretch across the plain, dotted with copses, farms and myriad church towers, to a ridge of hills clothed in conifers. These are the Formby Hills, a series of dunes and ridges stretching up along the coast towards Southport and a National Nature Reserve famed for red squirrels and natterjack toads. Bear left with the road and then right immediately past the terrace of cottages, following this track for several hundred yards until it bends off to the right. Ahead, the large gasometer marks the position of Southport, beyond this the famous tower at Blackpool and on the far horizon the hills of the southern Lake District.

Where the track bends right you should veer left and walk to the area of scrub oak, gorse bushes, bracken and brambles. Several paths leave this area, you want the one that leads steeply downhill and directly towards the spire of Halsall church some three miles distant; the path passes an isolated oak tree and follows the line of a ditch. Skirt the clump of willows to their left and, once round them, turn to face a further clump of willows on your left. Walk towards these for about 20 yards then turn right and walk to yet another clump. At these turn left and follow the developing track along to the minor road. Turn left and then follow this road round the right-angled bend and along to the farm. The barn on the right has a date stone of 1802 high up on the front wall.

At the road junction at this farm turn right along Narrow Lane and walk along to the next junction, here going straight on towards the hamlet of Bangor's Green. Where the road bends sharply right look for the obvious path just to the right of the chevrons and which follows the top of a dyke bank. Walk along this path with the dyke to your left, continue straight ahead at its end and keep the resultant ditch to your right. The path brings you to a bridge over the canal; cross this, walk down the steps to the towpath and turn right, the canal to your left. Remain now with the towpath to return to Lydiate about three miles away. The fields here are often host to vast flocks of pink-footed geese and ringed plover and patrolled by kestrel, sparrow hawk and fox. The canal winds past small villages and some large old farmhouses as well as two decent pubs, The Ship Inn at Haskayne and The Scarisbrick Arms Hotel at Downholland Cross. Remain on the towpath at bridge 19, passing opposite the winding hole and cottages mentioned earlier. At the next bridge climb the steps at the far side, cross the canal and turn right, retracing the path back to the road bridge. Regain the main road here and turn right to return to the pub.

10. South-West Lancashire: Croston

Route: Croston – Eccleston – Heskin Old Hall – Croston Moss

Distance: 6 miles

Map: Explorer 285, Southport & Chorley

Start: Lord Nelson, Croston, Preston PR26 9HJ

Access: Croston is on the A581 road about six miles west of Chorley. The Lord Nelson is at the heart of the village, facing the green to your right as you wind along the village's narrow main street. The village has a railway station on the line between Preston and Ormskirk with a regular service on Mondays to Saturdays (no Sunday trains) and connections to Liverpool Central at Ormskirk; it is about half a mile's walk from the pub.

Lord Nelson (01772 600387)

Named after the eponymous naval hero the pub was, before 1805, known as the Green Man. Its early history is uncertain but the thick, solid walls, beams and low ceilings suggest a respectable age. What is certain is that until after the second war the pub was an integral part of a village farmhouse; such dual use of a property was common in centuries past and many village alehouses first appeared as an offshoot of a farmer's, potter's, thatcher's or smith's business.

The one bar is the middle one of the three small rooms, each comfortably furnished and decorated with paintings and prints depicting scenes from the life and times of Horatio Nelson. The bar sports handpumps offering Boddingtons, Robinson's and Cains bitters, all excellently kept by the enthusiastic and knowledgeable landlords Don and Julie Baker. This is a very traditional pub with stone-flagged floor in the main bar. Outside there is a table and seating area and bowling green where team matches take place in evenings and friendly matches on Sundays.

Opening hours are Mon-Sat, noon – 11.00pm; Sun, noon – 10.30pm; the lounge/dining area is available for Sunday lunches (noon – 3.00pm); for the rest of the week, bar snacks are available in the bar area.

Croston

Substantial modern developments and infilling may have considerably increased its overall population in recent years but the ancient core of the village, along the winding main street and adjoining the green, has helped it retain its character. Old brick, stone and whitewashed cottages jumbled together are backed by barns and farmyards in a compact centre where an annual market and fair has been chartered since 1283.

The River Yarrow is channelled through the village in a deep, winding, stone trough although even this does not stop periodic floods inundating the village centre. A magnificent cobbled packhorse bridge dating from 1682 spans the river towards the eastern end of the main street; the view across this to Church Street and the askew tower of St Michael and All Angels church is virtually unaltered since the street was last rebuilt about 300 years ago. Originally founded in AD651 the church is typical of many in this part of Lancashire, its solid, mellow sandstone tower dominating the hori-

The Lord Nelson

zon. The churchyard also houses the village school, founded by John of Gaunt in 1372 although the contemporary building is somewhat younger.

The village lies towards the edge of the Lancashire Plain, bordered to the south by the low-lying Croston Moss, drained in the late-18th century to provide rich farmland. To the east the land rises slowly to the high West Pennines, source of the Yarrow which joins the River Douglas immediately west of Croston and thence flows to the Ribble Estuary some eight miles west of Preston. Little evidence remains of the pre-war industries which once made the village self sufficient; cotton mills, brickworks, feed mills and the gasworks have all vanished, only one animal feedstuffs mill survives to the east of the village. Mirroring this change, the number of pubs has been halved in the same period.

The Walk

Walk to the main road at the far end of the green from the pub and turn left along the main street. At the point where this bears sharp left, continue straight ahead past the old cross and along Church Street, entering the churchyard at the far end. Pass between the tower and the school and leave the churchyard at the green posts, following the river, to your right, upstream. Leave the meadow via the stile beside the low, white cottage and turn right along the minor road, Grape Lane, remaining with this until you reach a bridge across the Yarrow about half a mile distant. Do not cross this bridge but bear left just beforehand at the public footpath sign for Highfield Road and Eccleston, soon crossing a stile and thereafter remaining with the riverbank. The small weir marks the start of the mill leat, which once fed water to Croston Mill, still in operation on the far riverbank but no longer dependent on the river. Beside the weir is a small concrete shed with an aerial, this appears to be an automatic river gauge, feeding information to the local water company via radio waves, the power for the transmitter coming from a solar panel on the shed roof.

Remain with the river for the next mile or so; the path is well used and leads to the village of Eccleston. Walk in front of the cottages to the road and turn right, crossing the bridge and entering the edge of the village. Pass the Blue Anchor pub on your right and then turn right along Tincklers Lane. This skirts the north-western edge of

Eccleston and is somewhat windy and busy so care is counselled. At the T-junction turn right along the road, which retains the name Tincklers Lane, and remain with it for several hundred yards. Once past Tincklers Lane Cottage on your right cross to the left of the road and keep your eyes peeled for a stile well hidden in behind the line of the hedge. Cross this and follow the line of the hedge beyond virtually down to the stream, immediately before reaching which you should cross a stile on your left and, from here, follow the stream upstream for nearly half a mile.

On reaching the housing estate look for the footbridge across the stream – half-right across the meadow – and cross this, then the stile immediately beyond. Walk straight up the field ahead of you and then into the next field via any of the wide gaps in the old hedge. Here, head half-left and aim for the sheds and white cottage at the end of this field. Leave the field by the stile next to the farmyard gate and then follow the drive away from the cottage, Shelbourne House Farm, to the narrow road at the end, turning right along this, which soon deteriorates into a farm track. Pass two bungalows on your left and then take the footpath on the left, signposted to Halfpenny Lane. Keep to the left of the wooden sheds and enter the field at the end via the stile, walk ahead to the woods at the end and enter them over a further stile.

A roughly cobbled track leads down to a wooden footbridge across the stream at the bottom of this peaceful wooded dingle. Cross the bridge and follow the track ahead up the far side of the steep valley, remaining within the narrow band of trees until the path eventually emerges into the driveway of Heskin Old Hall, the solid stone farm to your left. Walk ahead along the drive to the minor road and turn right, then right again at the triangular green into Tannersmith Lane. Continue along here for about a third of a mile and turn left along Hand Lane – it's the first left turn you reach. At the far end turn right and walk for about 100 yards until you reach Robin Hood Cottage on your right, the stone plaque high on the wall dating it to 1889. Opposite this is Nook Lane, along which you wind for the next mile or so, following the footpath sign where appropriate towards Meadow Lane.

The road goes imperceptibly downhill, leaving the low, undulating countryside behind and leading down to Croston Moss. Bear right at the fork to walk between the farm on your left and the barns

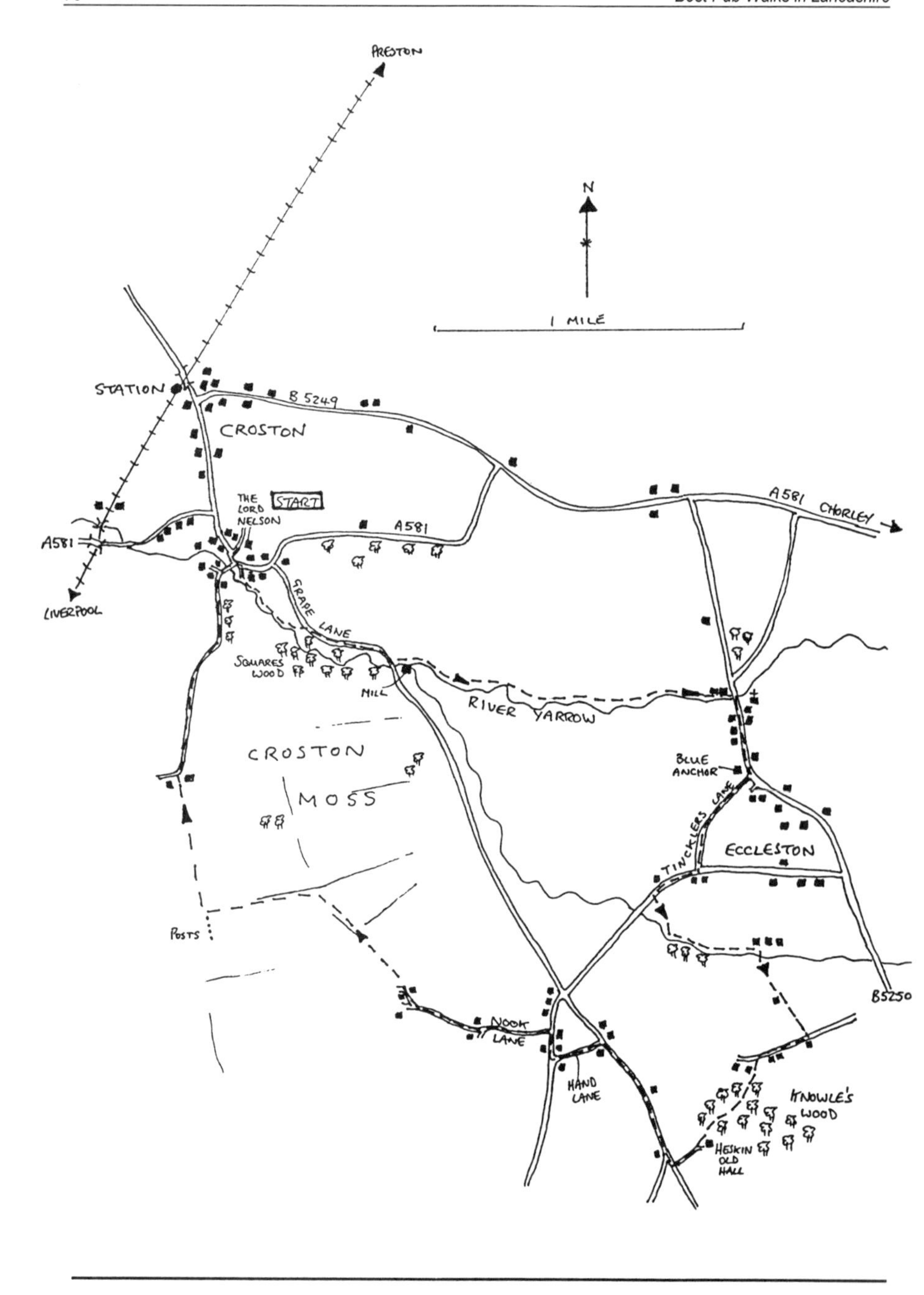
PRESTON
N
1 MILE
STATION
B 5249
CROSTON
THE LORD NELSON
START
A581
A581
LIVERPOOL
A581
CHORLEY
GRAPE LANE
SQUARES WOOD
MILL
RIVER YARROW
CROSTON
MOSS
BLUE ANCHOR
TINCKLERS LANE
ECCLESTON
POSTS
NOOK LANE
HAND LANE
B5250
KNOWLE'S WOOD
HESKIN OLD HALL

on your right; then where the track turns away to the left carry straight ahead, joining the line of a hedge on your left. Where the hedge peters out bear slightly left and walk along the line of the track, remaining with this for about a third of a mile and passing between fields of vegetables. The mossland is dotted with spinneys; ahead a long low ridge marks the site of Rufford village and the line of the railway. Pass by a ditch that comes in at a right angle from your right. Several hundred yards further on another ditch comes in at an acute angle from the right, at this point you should bear left and follow the ditch to a line of four wooden posts about 200 yards away.

Pause here to appreciate the views behind across the gentle countryside you've walked through to the distinct profile of Winter Hill, topped by transmitters, at the heart of the West Pennine Moors; to your left is nearby Harrock Hill and, virtually in line with the wooden posts, the obelisk on top of Ashurst's Beacon. From these poles turn right along the track and walk towards the farm and barns some distance away. Bear right as you reach the farm then almost immediately left and follow the by-now surfaced lane back to Croston. Turn right at the end, cross the packhorse bridge and then turn left to reach the green and The Lord Nelson.

11. South-West Lancashire: Dalton

Route: Walthew Park – Dean Wood – Gathurst – Leeds & Liverpool Canal – Appley Bridge – Ashurst's Beacon

Distance: 7.5 miles

Map: Explorer 285, Southport & Chorley

Start: The Prince William Inn, Beacon Lane, Dalton, Near Wigan WN8 7RU

Access: The pub is very close to Ashurst's Beacon, a prominent landmark some five miles west of Wigan. From Wigan, take the A577 through Orrell towards Skelmersdale, passing very close to Junction 26 on the M6. Go round the tight hairpin bend in Upholland and continue for about 400 yards to the Victoria Hotel on the right. The minor road immediately before this on the right, Mill Lane, leads along to the Prince William Inn, which is about half a mile past the country park and on the right.

By rail, you can pick up the walk at either Gathurst or Appley Bridge stations, both of which are on the regular, daily, Manchester to Southport (via Wigan Wallgate) service.

The Prince William Inn (01695 623989)

Ramblers with a Royalist bent will particularly appreciate this long established pub in a dominant position close to the summit of Ashurst's Beacon. In recent years, it has seen an extension and extensive redecoration but retains its weather-beaten old sign depicting Prince William, later the fourth King George who lived from 1765-1837. The open-plan pub is comfortably furnished and internal wall decorations reflect its name; there are family trees of the royal family since medieval times and paintings, photographs and mementoes of significant royal events in the past. The house beer comes from Burtonwood's brewery near Warrington, Burtonwood Best Bitter and several guest beers being available from a range of handpumps along the long bar which serves the one large room the pub offers. An adjoining room has been converted into a non-smoking restaurant.

Complementing the draught Burtonwood is a daily selection of bar snacks and meals, invariably offering a vegetarian option; food is available from Mon-Fri, noon – 2.30pm and 5.30 – 9.00pm; Sat, noon – 9.00pm and Sun, noon – 7.00pm. The pub itself is open all permitted hours and is a popular meeting place for rambling groups on this high ridge above industrial Lancashire. Children are actively encouraged – there is even a crazy golf course in the pub's beer garden.

Ashurst's Beacon

About 300 yards north of the pub and just behind the neighbouring Beacon Inn, Ashurst's Beacon is the highest point in the line of low hills which mark the end of the Lancashire Plain to the west and the first rumblings of the Pennines to the east. Both these features are easily visible from the top on a clear day from what is one of the best viewpoints in Lancashire; virtually the whole of the county is visible and those with binoculars should be able to discern up to four National Parks – The Lake District, Snowdonia, The Yorkshire Dales and The Peak District.

At around 580ft above sea level, a monument that is a cross between a tower and an obelisk crowns it. This was constructed in 1798 as one of a series of beacon towers built throughout the length and breadth of England at a time when invasion by Napoleon seemed a certainty, they were to act as early warnings of such an invasion. There is little doubt that similar use was made of this lofty perch over two centuries earlier when beacons were prepared to warn of the Spanish Armada in 1588. A short distance to the north-west of the hilltop is Ashurst's Hall, home to the family after which the hill is named; the poet Byron had connections with the family but whether he stayed in the area is unrecorded. The Beacon is part of Beacon Country Park, developed to benefit the residents of nearby Skelmersdale, a new town on the plain immediately west of the park. facilities include a visitor centre, nature trails and a golf course and driving range; these are off the ridge-top road about half a mile south of The Prince William.

The Walk

Leave the car park of the Prince William Inn and turn right along Beacon Lane. Almost immediately, turn right again into Long Heys Lane and walk along this for about 100 yards. At this point you reach

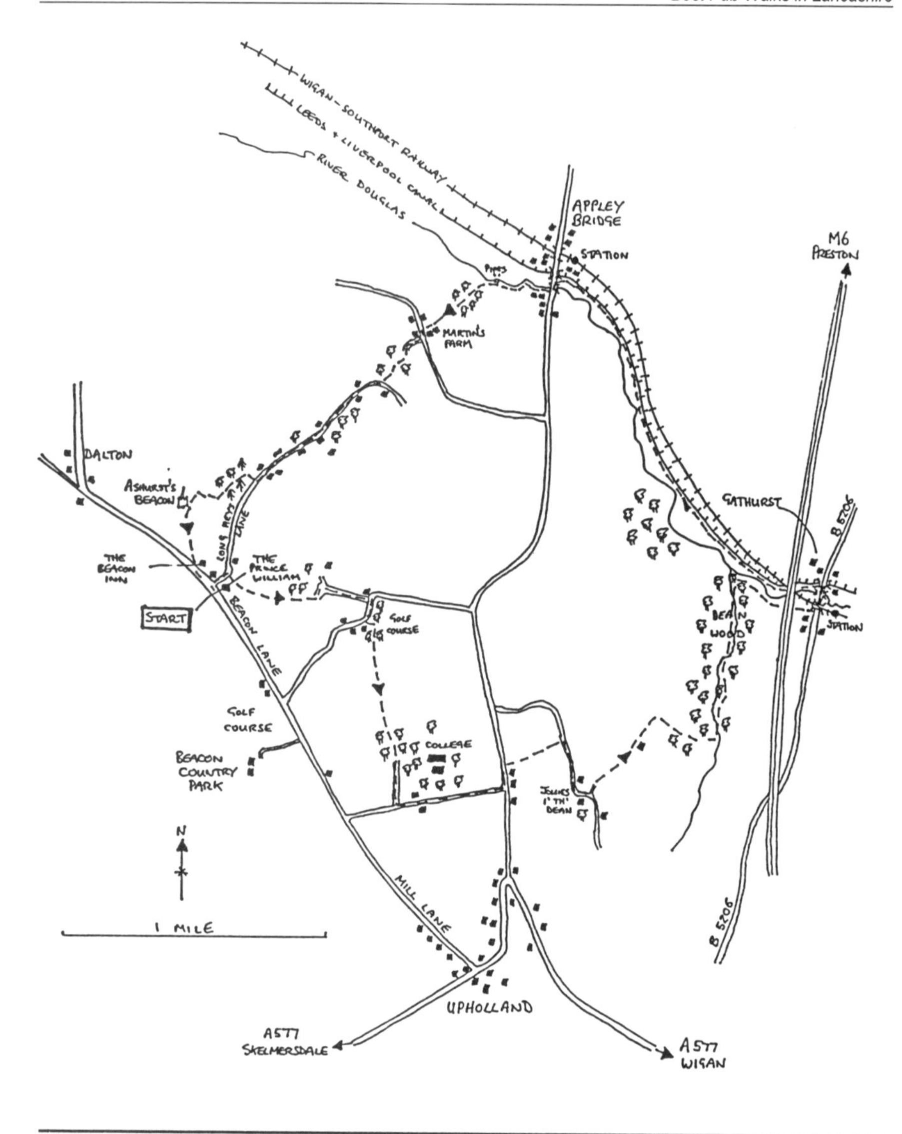

on your right the entrance to a rail-fenced car park, there is also a yellow waymark arrow nailed to a tree. Turn right here and stick to the right-hand edge, a rutted track developing almost immediately. Follow this track around, the car park petering out on the left whilst to the right is the village cricket pitch. As the track fails, continue straight ahead, sticking to the hedge on your left. At the gap, virtually opposite the thin wedge of trees, change to the other side of the hedge and walk downhill, keeping close to the hedge. At the bottom, join the rough road and turn left.

Visible some distance ahead of you is a fine old building, Stone Hall. You, however, should turn right at the triangular junction marked by a large ash tree and walk down along this rough road for about a quarter of a mile to the point where it issues onto a minor road in front of a red-roofed bungalow. Turn right here and walk along the straight. At the end of this straight, and immediately before the garage, a stile on the left, marked by a yellow hydrant plate, leads onto a small golf course. Climb this stile and walk directly forwards across the fairway, aiming for the tall ash tree in the woods beyond (as a further guide there are seven smaller trees growing in a line about five yards out from the far edge of the fairway, you need to pass to the right of the farthest-left tree). Walk virtually straight through the woods here, slightly favouring your right hand. At the far side, a large field opens out. You should remain just in the woods and turn right, following the indistinct path until it, too, leaves the woods at a point marked by a boulder.

The way now is straight on, keeping the hedge to your left until a rough track is gained, lined on the right by an infilled quarry. Walk along this track, rich in wildflowers from spring to late autumn, bearing left where necessary as you walk through the oak and beech woodlands. At the T-junction at the end of the track turn left and walk downhill through the area of farm buildings to join a surfaced road, passing a red brick house on your right. Hidden in the trees on the left is the substantial St Joseph's College in Walthew Park, once a seminary for training Catholic priests but now a College of Theology.

At the bottom turn left along the main road, cross it and about 20 yards beyond the last bungalow turn right into the field, following the line of telegraph poles down the gentle slope. There is a small stone quarry being worked on your right so don't be alarmed to hear explosions from time to time. Forming the horizon ahead is a long, low line of hills to the north of Wigan, part of the large Haigh Country Park; nearer to hand is the M6 Motorway and the massive H.J. Heinz factory. On reaching the minor road turn right and follow it for about a third of a mile, bearing sharp left and going downhill to a sharp right-hand bend at Jollies i'th' Dean Farm. At this spot is a small duck pond populated by a variety of duck and geese, some wooden huts in the trees and an immense number of "domestic" rabbits hopping about the area.

Here turn left up the drive dedicated to Dean Wood Farm. Follow the track past several stables and stock-rearing sheds on your right to the point where the fence ends and a public footpath sign points right. Take this path, remaining outside the wire and follow the obvious path down into the trees just as the woods close in at the corner of the field. A steep scramble down over natural sandstone steps and ledges brings you to the stream that flows through these quiet, peaceful woodlands, Dean Woods. Shortly you will come to two footbridges, one metal, one wooden. Cross the metal one and bear left uphill at the far side, following the path up through the woods. Bear right at the fork to emerge at the woodland edge beside a barbed wire fence. To you right is a stile, cross this and turn left to follow the woodland edge.

Passing through a further stile on your left, continue forward but this time on the woodland side of the fence, working gradually down into the woods to pick up a more obvious track running high above the deepening valley. Walk right down this path, crossing fallen trees and passing massive bracket fungi adorning dead tree stumps. You reach the stream at some rough stepping stones, decidedly slippery and undoubtedly underwater after prolonged heavy rain. Cross the stream here, which marks the Lancashire/Greater Manchester boundary, and continue downstream, keeping the main watercourse to your right, fording a further two side streams before crossing the green footbridge that appears on your right. Follow the track away left from this and emerge from the woodland on the valley floor of the River Douglas.

Ahead, the massive viaduct that carries the M6 70ft above the river dominates the view. To the left, the Leeds and Liverpool Canal and the Wigan to Southport railway follow the river through this deep, winding section of valley. Remain with the track, pass beneath the viaduct and walk to the end to join the B5206 road near Gathurst station. Turn left, pass under the railway and cross the river bridge, then look for the blue cycleway sign pointing left towards Burscough; following the direction of this sign takes you down to the canal towpath not far from the Navigation Pub.

Ashurst's Beacon

For the next mile and a half, stick with the towpath, the canal to your right. There's an impressive view of the M6 crossing high over the railway line which, in turn, passes low over the canal, the river just off to the left. Beyond this the lock keepers cottage at Dean Locks is passed by on a long, cobbled section of towpath, just remain to the left of the canal and wind round the back of the cottage. A very scenic part of the walk now follows, the sound of the M6 dying off and the canal winding along the contour about 20ft above the river, all well wooded and with views ahead to Parbold Hill. Pause at the second swing bridge you come to and look directly left to see the obelisk atop Ashurst's Beacon, your destination still several miles distant.

On reaching Appley Bridge leave the towpath and turn left down the road, almost immediately crossing the river bridge. Straightaway, look on the right for a narrow path threading along between the cottages and the river and walk along this, cottage gardens and allotments to your left. Stay with the riverbank until you have passed the collection of large pipes that cross and/or stand upright by the river. A short, broken section of fencing is immediately ahead of you whilst to your left, beyond some concrete slabs, is a truncated hedge. Walk across the field to this hedge and then follow its line, keeping it to your left. Where it finishes, walk straight forward to the brook and narrow strip of woodland. There is a crossing place just to your right here; cross the brook then turn left, following the obvious path as it winds up through the woodland. Emerging from these woods a large renovated house and quasi-detached garage are on your left; the definitive right of way skirts the very edge of the garden straight ahead to emerge onto a narrow road next to the small electricity transformer, located as Martins Farm.

Turn left along this road and then take the rough lane on the right just past the cottages, following this as it winds gently uphill. At the point where it splits three ways, you should take the narrow middle option. Follow the path along to a stream, cross this and then walk up the far bank, the path here and there using natural rock steps to gain height. On reaching the minor road turn right and follow it uphill, ignoring the track that almost immediately branches off to the right.

After about half a mile pass by the renovated Catteralls Farm and barn off to your left. Wind round the bends above this and keep your eyes peeled for a gap in the high bank to your right – it's directly opposite where the spinney on your left peters out to a point. Go up through this gap and climb to the field. Stick with the right-hand edge and follow it round until you see a footbridge down in the deep wooded clough on your right. Cross this, and the stile beyond, and turn left, walking up the left-hand edge of the field to a further stile near the top beside a five-barred gate. Cross this and walk on into the woodland, then after about 200 yards take any one of the tracks on your right up through the trees to reach the monument on top of Ashurst's Beacon. Ahead of you, far below, is Skelmersdale. Walk along the ridge with the town down to your right, cross the stile and follow the track down along to the minor road. Turn left up this, pass the Beacon Inn and return to the Prince William Inn about 200 yards further on.

12. The Fylde: Elswick

Route: Elswick – Crossmoor – Wharles – Medlar – Scholar Bridge

Distance: 7 miles

Map: Explorer 286, Blackpool & Preston

Start: The Ship Hotel, Elswick

Access: From Blackpool take the A586 road towards Garstang, Lancaster and M6 (North). Turn right at the major junction east of Little Singleton and go south along the A585 towards Kirkham, the M55, Preston and M6(South). After about a mile turn left along the B5269 towards Longridge. Turn first left and on reaching Elswick keep right with the main road. The Ship is on the right. From Preston, join the M55 towards Blackpool. Take the junction for Fleetwood (A585) and head north for about 2 miles. Elswick is signposted off to the right.

The Ship Hotel (01995 670131)

In the midst of the Fylde, Elswick retains much of the character of its origins as a small farming community, with plenty of old cottages, village centre farms and imposing yeoman's houses. At the heart of the community is the Ship Hotel, a substantial roadside inn set in large grounds. It's a long and surprisingly low pub, basically open plan but with enough nooks and crannies to make it interesting. A large, pot-bellied stove draws the eye to one end, where a dedicated dining area is located (note that larger walking parties can book to have breakfast here!). A substantial collection of old stone and glass bottles fills shelves and crevices, whilst country and sporting prints dot the walls. Wall-bench seating and a rag-tag mix of seats and tables add character to the beamed interior; there is also a separate pool room.

It's a Pubmaster-owned pub, with the main hand-pulled beer being their standard Boddingtons Bitter. The busier summer months see additional guest beers added to the range. There are also the usual suspects in the lager, stout and cider field. To the front are a few hanging baskets, walled gardens and beds, but it is to the rear where the pub scores highly, with a cosy beer garden backed by a large grassy play area with climbing frames, etc. to keep the kids amused. The Ship is open every day from 11am to 11pm (12 noon-10.30pm Sundays); food (everything from snacks to full a la carte menu) is available between noon – 2pm and 5pm – 9pm (all day weekends and summer).

The Fylde

Picture an area that was scraped flat and clean by glaciers 12000 years ago. When the ice retreated it left mounds and ridges of sands and gravels standing out from a plain covered with boulder clay and dank marshes, the whole rarely more than a few feet above sea level and well wooded. This is the landscape the Romans found when they claimed the area two thousand years ago. They built a port at the now lost Portus Stetenorium (assumed to be somewhere near present day Kirkham and a victim of the shifting coastline in this area, no positive remains have been found) but did little to change the surrounding countryside. The original native settlers gave us the name of the area. Fylde is derived from the Old English "gefilde" meaning, simply, "plain," and includes the coastline, salt marshes, estuaries and low lands between the Lune in the north and the Ribble in the south.

Only in the late-18th and 19th centuries did the Fylde we know today come into being. The neat areas of woodland, spinneys and copses that break up the landscape, the isolated farmsteads nestling on almost every slight hummock or ridge in the area and the compact local villages are largely a product of the era of the land drainers. These were a breed of engineers and visionaries who used wind power to help drain the vast areas of marsh, mossland and thick clayey soils, creating a complex network of drainage channels and resulting in very rich farmland underlain by hundreds of miles of clay field drains. There was even a patron saint of underdrainers, St Eloi! Only a handful of the hundreds of windmills that once characterised the Fylde now remain, none used for their original purpose.

The Fylde is probably best known today for the holiday resorts at Blackpool and Lytham – St Anne's, none of which was more than a few fishermen's huts until well into the Victorian era, and for Fleetwood, essentially a failed railway company resort town which developed into one of the top fishing ports in Britain before reces-

Elswick

sion virtually destroyed this industry. If these rather brash places are your idea of the Fylde then put aside this prejudice for a day or two and try the suggested walks which are guaranteed to offer you a fresh perspective on Blackpool's back door; undemanding, peaceful and packed with interest for nature lovers.

The Walk

(Note that the green lane beyond Medlar Hall may have deep mud after heavy rain.)

Face the front of The Ship and take the gap on the left, passing beside the pub and along a narrowish path that soon emerges into a grassy area in front of housing. Turn left here, putting the swings on your right. Go straight over two estate roads and continue ahead, soon passing a former hauliers yard on your left. At the end, Roseacre Lane, turn left and walk to the crossroads. Go straight across and walk to Bonds Ice Cream Parlour at the far end, here turning right along Bonds Lane (if you look left at this point you'll see the Boot and Shoe pub). Walk along for some distance to reach, on your right, a signboard for some kennels. On your left at this juncture, a

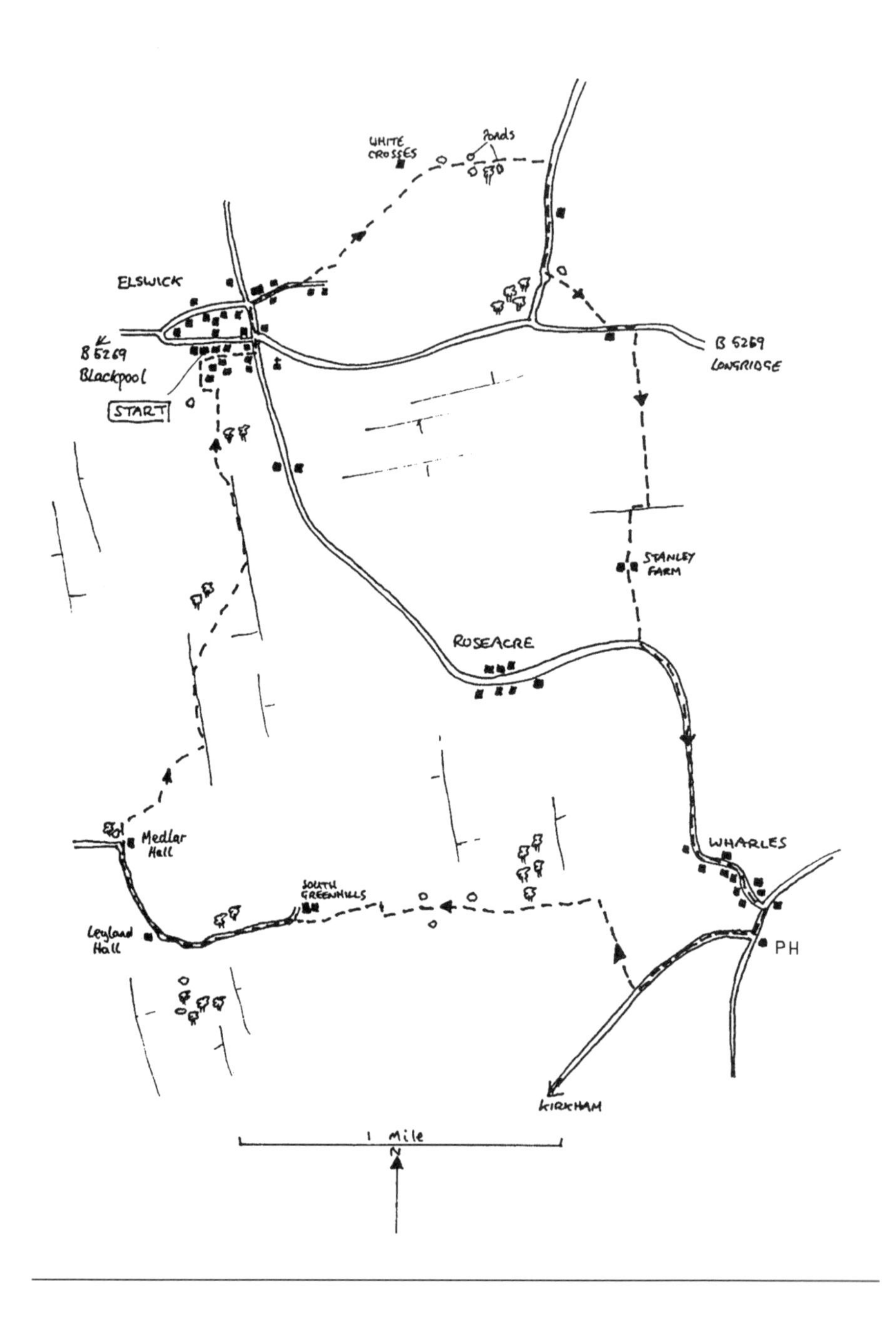
WHITE CROSSES
Ponds
ELSWICK
B 5269
Blackpool
START
B 5269
LONGRIDGE
STANLEY FARM
ROSEACRE
WHARLES
PH
Medlar Hall
SOUTH GREENHILLS
Leyland Hall
KIRKHAM
1 Mile
N

public footpath sign signals your route. Follow the well-trodden path across the field, cross the stile and walk ahead to the next stile just beyond the black drain cover. Once over this aim for the far left corner of the field and negotiate the rickety stile. Walk virtually straight ahead, keeping to the left of the field and heading towards the isolated cottage.

Ignore the stile on your left that would take you to this cottage and walk on to the end of the field, crossing the small bridge here. Aim now towards the right-hand clump of scrubby trees ahead of you, passing en route on your left a pond surrounded by trees and bushes. You should arrive at a stile over a fence on a narrow neck of land between two further ponds. Cross the stile and bear right, following the fence along past the spinney and, eventually, to a minor road. Turn right along this road.

Pass the farm and stick with the road until the obvious kink. Here, take the stile beneath the two trees on your left and aim for the farm across the field, leaving via the white gate at the far side. Turn left along the road here and walk for about 100 yards to the point where the road bends to the right. At this point look on the right for a well-hidden stile, cross this and walk with the line of fence across the paddock. Cross the stile at the far side and walk to the offset corner of the field not far ahead. Here cross the stile into the large field and keep the consequent line of hedge on your right for a further three fields to reach a footbridge. Cross this and turn right to follow the ditch for about 100 yards, then look directly left across the field to a farm gate. Walk across to this and pass through it (the right of way which lies some way to the left of this gate is blocked by a hedge, local practice seems to be to use this gate as an alternative) and then follow the track beyond to the farmyard. Go straight through the yard and along the drive at the far side, following this to the minor road at the end. Turn left along the road here, tracing this usually peaceful lane to and through the hamlet of Wharles. Turn right at the T-junction to reach the Eagle and Child pub (restricted opening hours).

Turn right and walk along the road directly opposite the pub, Moorside, following the sign for Kirkham. Go round the bend and start to climb slowly uphill. About 100 yards before the top of the rise are two field gates on opposite sides of the road. You should go through the one on the right, bear right to the hedge and follow the line of this away from the road for the length of two fields. At the end of the second field, you will find some gates at the end of a lane. Go through the gate out of the field and then cross the stile beside the gate ahead of you, turning left and following the line of the hedge. Pass the end of the woodland and carry on along with the line of the fence. From the point where this turns right walk straight ahead across the field heading towards the farm you can see in the distance (N.B. not the farm off to your left), South Greenhills.

On this line of sight, continue across a series of stiles to reach a footbridge over a drainage ditch. Cross this, turn right and walk to the hedge, whereupon turn left and follow its line up across two fields. Go through the gate at the end and then through the gate immediately on your left (do not go down the farm track). Turn right and follow the field boundary in front of the garden of the farm. Cross the stile at the end and turn right up to the surfaced road, then turn left along this. Remain with this as it winds around and bends sharp right past the farm called Leyland Hall. Off to the left is a low marshy area with a number of ponds teeming with wildfowl; this walk passes a large number of such areas, some are natural, some marl holes dug by farmers in the past. At the next sharp left turn, marked by a copse of trees around a pond, go straight on and down the green lane ahead; to the right is Medlar Hall Farm. Pass through a gate across the track and follow this winding, sometimes very muddy, track right to its end where it peters out completely at the corner of a field by an old wooden shack.

From the corner near the shack walk along the edge of the field following the right-hand boundary, pass through a field gate and walk ahead to a footbridge across a field drain. Do not cross this bridge but instead turn left and follow the line of the drain along the edge of the pasture. At the end of the field cross the substantial concrete-slab footbridge, known locally as Scholar Bridge, and then bear half-right across the narrow field to join the line of another drain, then following this up the edge of this long field. Pass a stand of trees on your left and continue to the far end of the field. At the rough hedge here turn left and walk to the corner of the field to the stile marked by a boulder. Climb over the stile and then keep the hedge to your right, walking up to a narrow gap stile beside a field gate and then along the edge of another long field, passing the end of a farm track as you do so.

Once past this track look ahead to the far boundary hedge and aim to meet this roughly half way across, in line with the gabled terraced houses in the distance. Cross the footbridge at this point and walk ahead to the top end of the field. On reaching the fenced gardens turn left to gain a stile. Climb this, turn right and walk to the field corner. Pass through the kissing gate and go ahead (*not* along the road) along the footpath on the green swathe between the houses. When you reach the swings, turn left along the narrow path back to The Ship.

13. The Fylde: Glasson

Route: Conder Green – Glasson – Crook Farm – Cockersand Abbey – Hillam – Thurnham

Distance: 7.5 miles

Map: Explorer 296, Lancaster, Morecambe & Fleetwood

Start: The Stork Hotel, Conder Green, Near Lancaster LA2 0AN.

Access: The hamlet of Conder Green is about four miles south of Lancaster on the A588 road to Cockerham and Blackpool, The Stork Inn adjoins the main road. Alternatively a minor road from the crossroads in the centre of Galgate – on the A6 and just north of junction 33 on the M6 – is signposted to Conder Green (turn off the A6 by the Green Dragon and bear left just after the viaduct). The Stork is at the end of this minor road where it joins the A588.

The Stork Hotel (01524 751234)

This is a great pub to be at on a cold, almost still, winter morning when the marshes are at their best, wraith-like mists rising from the channels which thread the area, the eerie echoes and calls of unseen flights of wading birds and the gaunt ribs of rotting boats rising from the mudbanks, ephemeral in the drifting fog.

A pub has stood at the edge of the sea marsh here for at least 330 years; mention of it was made in a document recording local celebrations to mark the restoration to the throne of Charles II in 1660. In those days it was known as The Cocks, believed to reflect strong local interest in the then-popular pastime of cock fighting. By 1807, the long, low, oak panelled pub was named Duke Hamilton's Arms after the local Lord of the Manor. One of the Hamilton family houses was Ashton Hall, a mile to the north of the pub. The same Hamilton family had as a member a certain Emma, Lady Hamilton. It is said that Nelson once moored off Glasson and hired a renowned local river pilot, a blind man, to help him reach the said Lady at Ashton Hall via the treacherous channels through the marshes at the dead of night. The Hall still exists as the centre-piece of a golf course and country club.

The Stork, Conder Green

The name of the pub comes from the bird that is included in the crest of the Starkie family of Padiham who purchased the Ashton Estate in the 19th century. You will not see storks on the marshes that front the pub but you may well see swans, shellduck, pink-footed and Canada geese and a wide variety of wading birds. Other regular visitors include gypsies who stop on pastures near The Stork en route to and from the famous Appleby Horse Fair early each June; the colourful horse-drawn caravans and impromptu entertainments are a big attraction.

The year-round attraction at the pub is, however, the range of beers – Boddingtons and a range of guest beers served in comfortable surroundings by landlords Mr & Mrs Cragg and their extremely friendly staff. The brass and copper festooned snug has a great roaring fire in winter. A range of bar snacks is available (look for the specials written on the blackboard) and there is a special children's menu.

Outside the pub has a well-appointed play area for children and beer garden. One hopes this will not suffer from salt pollution as the pub is occasionally completely isolated for several hours each side of high tide at the spring and autumn neaps and by occasional storm tides. Opening hours, tides allowing, are Mon-Sat, 11.00am –

11.00pm; Sun, noon – 10.30pm. Food is served Mon-Fri, noon – 2.30pm and 6.00 – 9.00pm; Sat, noon – 2.30pm and 6.00 – 9.30pm and Sunday, noon – 9.00pm.

Glasson

Echoes of times past hang heavy in the air at this windswept, estuarine village that still, surprisingly, thrives in an age which has seen most similar places all-but die. Glasson's dock was developed to serve nearby Lancaster, itself a port used by seagoing vessels but prone to silting and reached only by a treacherous approach channel. The dock is at the end of a short branch of the Lancaster Canal that opened in 1799, eventually linking Preston with Kendal. The Glasson Dock branch opened in 1826 and connected the already existing dock to the canal network, ensuring a rapid escalation in its fortunes at the expense of Sunderland (see North Lune section) that became a ghost port; Lancaster Port (including Glasson) was ranked as the fourth busiest British port during the first half of the 19th century.

The coming of the railway marked the start of a slow decline of Glasson as a port. Although linked by rail to Lancaster in 1883, earlier rail lines to Fleetwood and to Heysham, both rapidly developing harbours only a few miles from Glasson, had started to milk trade away, both passenger and freight vessels preferring the facilities at these other ports. Glasson, however, refused to die and developed a modest shipbuilding and dry dock facility whilst continuing to receive coastal traders. This resilience helped Glasson survive the withdrawal of its passenger rail service as long ago as 1930 (the line was completely closed by the Beeching axe); in the last 25 years it has developed as a marina both for sea-going yachts and cruisers and canal craft. The dock itself remains in operation with regular shipments of timber from Scandinavia and some container and coaster work. It has also acted as a half-way house for old packet steamers; the Victoria Hotel has more than a few times been dwarfed by old passenger ferries on their final journey to the breakers yard.

Cockersand Abbey

Hugh Garth was something of a local celebrity in his day. In the time of the early Normans, he was treated as a saintly recluse, admired for his prowess at healing and benevolence to those in need. He lived in a hut overlooking the sands and rock ledges and became known as Hugh the Hermit. His interests and skills were developed by his successors at the site who had established a refuge for lepers and a sanatorium for monks by the year 1200. This later grew into Cockersand Abbey, one of the major Lancashire Houses and leading seminary of the Premonstratensian (White Canons) persuasion, famed for their medical training. That its fame spread far and wide is undoubted, records exist of a pier/jetty being built to cater for trade, passengers and pilgrims travelling to/from Ireland. A lighthouse was constructed, one of the earliest in these islands. The Reformation, however, put paid to the abbey; many of its stones were used in marshland farms and now only the small, weather-beaten chapter-house and a few piles of stone remain on this windswept foreshore. The chapter-house has, in the past, seen use as a mausoleum by the Dalton family of Thurnham and is thus kept locked.

The Walk

From the inn's door turn right along the narrow road and follow it to the car park and picnic site at the former Conder Green railway station. From here turn left to follow the old track-bed curving south on its embankment, well above the salt marshes and intricate meandering channels of the tiny River Conder as it meets the Lune estuary. Follow the old railway through to Glasson, leaving it near the Victoria Hotel and cross the swing bridge across the canal between the bustling marina and the Dock itself.

Walk uphill with the road, Tithebarn Hill, to the top and bear left. This is an excellent spot to stop and take in the views; at all of 65ft high it is one of the highest points in the whole of the Fylde. Ahead across the Lune is the lonely Sunderland Peninsular, behind you the heights of Bowland brood darkly beyond the modernist white architecture (it is supposed to mirror an Italian hill village) of Lancaster University. At your feet Glasson, further afield manmade features such as Blackpool Tower, Heysham nuclear power station and the gas platforms in Morecambe Bay. To your right, on a clear day, the mountains of the Lake District seem near enough to touch.

Descend the hill to the sharp left-hand bend and here take the right-hand-most track, Marsh Lane, which wends its way past a caravan park and down onto the boggy levels of Glasson Marsh. Simply remain with the line of track across the muddy fields to reach Crook

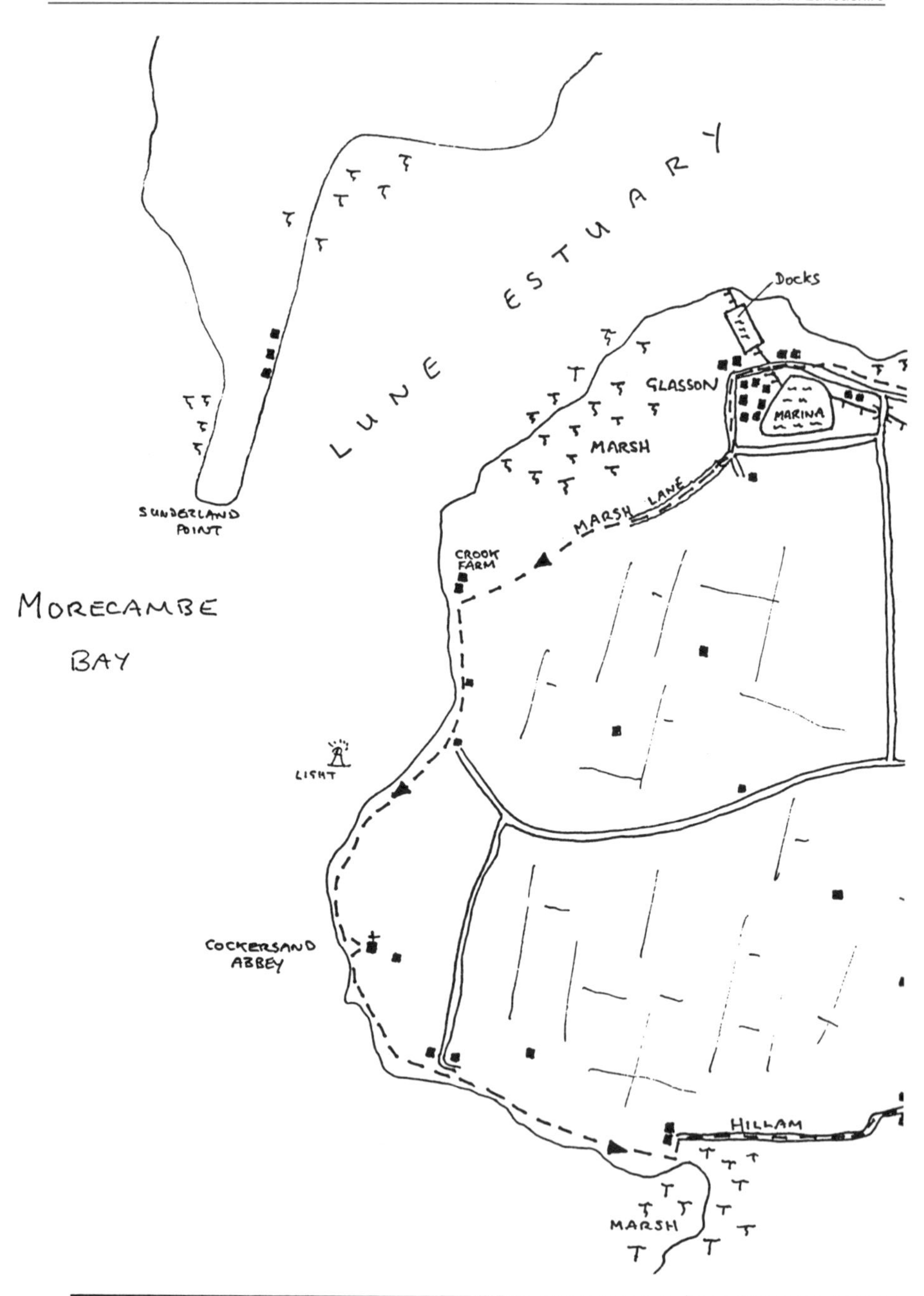

LUNE ESTUARY
Docks
GLASSON
MARINA
MARSH
MARSH LANE
SUNDERLAND POINT
CROOK FARM
MORECAMBE BAY
LIGHT
COCKERSAND ABBEY
HILLAM
MARSH

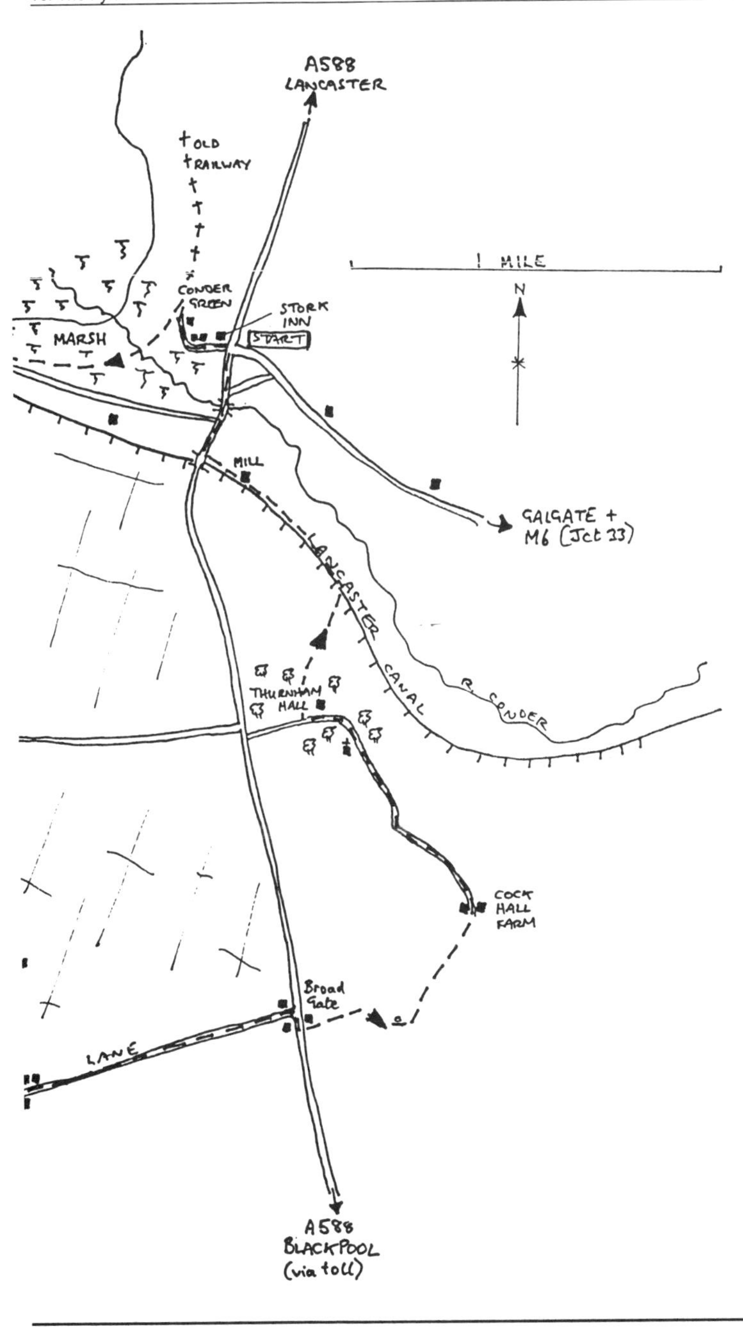
A588
LANCASTER
OLD
RAILWAY
1 MILE
N
CONDER
GREEN
STORK
INN
START
MARSH
MILL
GALGATE +
M6 (Jct 33)
LANCASTER
CANAL
R. CONDER
THURNHAM
HALL
COCK
HALL
FARM
Broad
Gate
LANE
A588
BLACKPOOL
(via toll)

Farm, pass through the gate to the left of the buildings here and turn left along the sea wall. This is an excellent place to walk following a winter's storm, beachcombing the rocky, pebbly foreshore can produce all sorts of surprises.

Continue south along the seashore, passing by the old lookout tower and Abbey Lighthouse Cottage; the derivation of the name is obvious but the pylon has seen better days. Out across the mudflats Plover Scar Light, at the seaward edge of a shelf of sandstone, marks the start of the channel to Glasson Dock and Lancaster. At low water, the flats are often busy with carts, tractors and a variety of other vehicles driven there by local shellfish gatherers who are harvesting the local cockle and mussel beds. Be wary of gathering your own, however – take note of the local warning signs. Instead, leave the collecting to the regulars and to the abundance of seabirds that prompted the designation of the whole area as a wildfowl refuge back in 1963.

In a short while a minor diversion from the coastal path allows you to reach the scant remains of Cockersand Abbey. Return to the coast and continue along the path, turning east to pass by Bank Houses and a caravan park on your left. Pass the next group of buildings, Bank End Farm, and join the narrow Hillam Lane, skirting the edge of the marsh and following it over a low ridge to reach the A588 road.

Turn right, then almost immediately look for the track just beyond Broad Gate Farm on your left – go through the middle one of three gates by the tumbledown shed. Go along the track from here and cross the stile at the end. Walk up along the greenway between the trees, then following the hedge on your right. When you reach the field gate between two stone posts pass through it and walk virtually straight ahead to reach the high point of the field, marked by trees. There's a duck pond at the top here; pass this to your left and look for the simple stile over the fence ahead just beyond the tall oak tree. Cross this and turn left downhill to reach two gates. Go through the right-hand one of these, walk through this small corral and on to the end of the track by an octagonal concrete water trough. Go through the gate here and head slightly left, aiming for the concentration of farm buildings visible ahead at Cock Hill Farm. Cross the intervening hedge and stream via the footbridge and aim for the gate near the two small silos visible in the farmyard. Enter the yard via the gate here and bear left around the barn supporting these silos, passing by a larger barn on your left. Walk straight ahead through the yard and leave the complex past a very large barn on your right (this is not strictly the definitive right of way but the one recommended by the lady of the farm).

You are now on a long farm drive, wind along with it for the next mile or so. On the left you will pass the church of St Thomas and Elizabeth that serves the scattered community of this, Thurnham; a fine mausoleum adjoins the church tower. Continue along the drive until you reach Thurnham Hall on your right. This is the ancestral home of the Dalton family; parts of it date back to the 13th century.

Turn right to walk down along the track in front of the hall and continue to the area of old barns on your right. Bear right past the back of these and, where the new rough road bears sharp right, turn left and walk to the old ruined barn. From here, follow the sunken, tree-lined greenway for a number of yards to reach a stile beside a green gate. Climb the stile and bear half-right to reach a bridge across the Glasson Dock branch of the Lancaster Canal. Walk across this and look carefully on your left before you leave the bridge to find the gap stile giving access to the towpath. Walk along the towpath, water to your left, passing some of the locks and reaching Thurnham Mill, an old corn mill whose long-gone machinery was once powered by water from the canal. Continue to the road bridge and leave the towpath here, heading north back to the Stork that is visible in the distance.

14. The Fylde: Cuddy Hill

Route: Cuddy Hill – Lancaster Canal – Woodplumpton – Bell Fold

Distance: 5 miles

Map: Explorer 286, Blackpool & Preston

Start: The Plough at Eaves, Cuddy Hill, Preston PR4 0BJ

Access: This is reputedly the most difficult pub in Lancashire to find, so if you have difficulty the Grid Reference is SD 494375. Take the A6 north from Preston to the traffic lights at Broughton and here turn left along the B5269 towards Elswick. Wind along with this for a little over a mile and turn right at the junction, remaining with the B5269. At the end of the short straight, turn right along the minor road signposted to Eaves and Barton. Cross the canal and, at the junction, turn left towards Eaves. Simply keep left to arrive at the pub about a mile along on your right.

The Plough at Eaves (01772 690233)

The pub appears to be named after a local farm, the actual postal address of Cuddy Hill refers to a wide area of scattered cottages and farms here some five miles north-west of Preston. The Plough dates back as a pub to 1625, obviously a period when the average stature was somewhat more restricted than today – anyone much over 6ft tall will have difficulty straightening up inside this low, heavily beamed building. It stands on the site of the Battle of Cuddy Hill which was fought in 1546, one of many skirmishes in the long-drawn out conflict between the Tudors and the Scots. A century later the pub was used as a refuge by both Royalist and Parliamentarian troops at the time of the Battle of Preston; can't you just picture the landlord forever turning around a double-sided picture of Cromwell and Charles I, depending on which way the tide of battle was flowing?

Sadly, no such picture survives. There are, however, a lot of old prints depicting the Civil War era which the previous landlord, David Atherton, unearthed during alterations and extensions to the building. These alterations have provided an extension to the restaurant business of the pub but left the bar area materially unchanged. The tiled floor is dotted with solid chairs and tables, complemented by comfortable wall seats both in the main bar area and the tiny side room. A feature of the pub is a large fireplace, the chimneybreast of which is decorated with a number of old flintlock shotguns. Elsewhere the ubiquitous horse brasses and varieties of copper and brass ornaments are at home in the timeless atmosphere of the room. Two people tired of this atmosphere 20 years ago, however; the ghost of an old lady and child appeared regularly from the 1750s until 1980 when the pub last underwent alterations – perhaps they didn't approve, although it's hard to imagine why.

Once a free house, the Plough is now tied to Thwaites brewery. The pub is closed on Monday during the day, but open in the evening and then all day Tue-Sun. Food is available between noon – 2.30pm and 6.15pm – 9.15pm, Tue-Sat and on Sunday from noon – 8.45pm. Renowned for Sunday lunch specials such as shoulder of lamb and the "Plough Whale" – a fish dish reflecting the size of the haddock served!

The Walk

Walk down the right side of the pub and through to the back of the car park beyond, cross the stile here and walk along the line of the fence on the right of the narrow pasture. Cross the stile about half way along this fence and turn left, crossing a further two stiles to emerge on a minor road at the top of the bungalow's garden. Cross virtually straight over and enter the field opposite through the gate to the left of the black wooden barn. Walk ahead towards the middle of the hedge across the far end of the field, cross the small, overgrown footbridge and follow the line of hedge on your right, aiming for the isolated red brick house. Cross the stile and walk up the right-hand side of the house, go through the gate at the front and turn right along the drive.

Walk along this past further houses on your right, cross through the rickety gate and continue along the green track beyond. At the end of the first field on your left is a stile, climb this and walk ahead across the field to the towpath of the Lancaster Canal, turning right along this. The canal is your companion for the next mile or so, lined here and there with trees or tall rushbeds and heavily populated by all sorts of water birds. Even in summer this canal is peaceful,

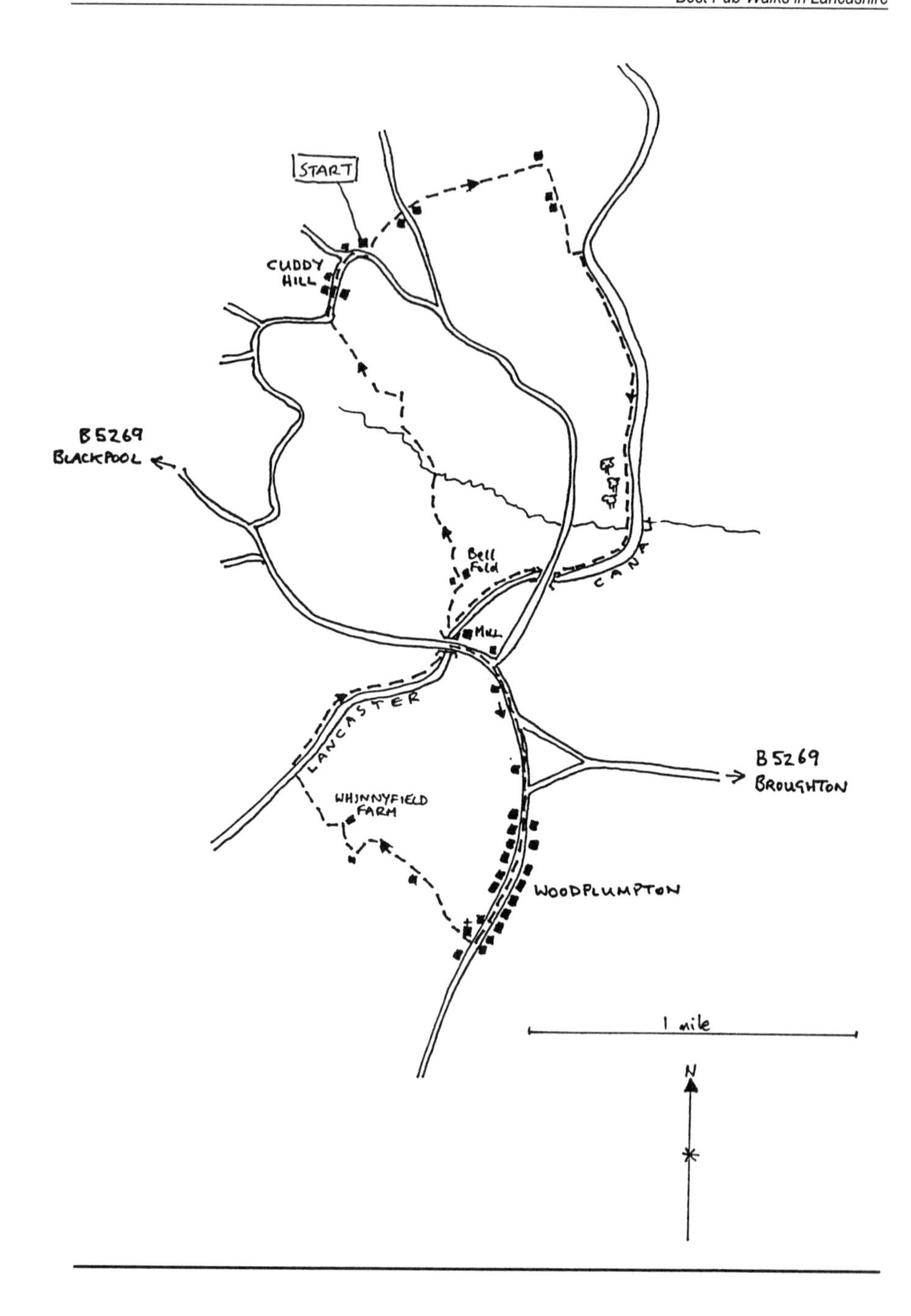
START
CUDDY HILL
B5269
BLACKPOOL
Bell Fold
MILL
CANAL
LANCASTER
B5269
BROUGHTON
WHINNYFIELD FARM
WOODPLUMPTON
1 mile
N

largely because it is landlocked (it always has been, plans to link it to the Ribble in Preston never came to fruition). Views off to your left encompass Longridge Fell, the southern fells of The Forest of Bowland and the outlying, wooded, Beacon Fell. Remain on the towpath until you reach the bridge next to the feed mill, climb off the towpath here and then cross the bridge, walking along with the main road into the village of Woodplumpton.

Woodplumpton

This long linear village is no more than a veneer on each side of the Preston road; it is recorded in Domesday but few of the buildings in today's village can claim a long history. An exception is St Anne's church, a curious mixture of trim, Georgian style architecture and much older, weather-beaten sandstone that may date back to the 13th century. The village stocks remain in place just outside the lychgate, next door is a farm dated 1702 and opposite is the village pub The Wheatsheaf. A curious burial in the churchyard is that of Meg Shelton, the Fylde witch. She was a local villager, Margery Hilton, who had been saddled with a tarnished and unholy reputation. When she died in 1705 she was buried at the dead of night but, come the following morning, had scratched her way out of her grave. A second burial met with the same result so the third attempt included the variation of burying her face-down and capping the grave with a large boulder. This has apparently worked as the boulder remains undisturbed beside a path in the churchyard.

The walk leaves the village via the churchyard. Walk west through the churchyard, passing Meg's grave on your left and turn right at the crossing of paths. Climb down through the gap in the graveyard wall at the end of this path and walk ahead and slightly left, picking up the hedge on your right. Walk along through the fields, keeping the hedge to your right. At the end of the fields go through the gate and turn left along the drive, winding round with it and passing two houses on your left to reach the farmyard at Whinnyfield Farm. Walk up the farmyard past the barn on your left and the bullpen to your right and, at the far end, turn left along the muddy track. Go through the gate, pass the barn to your left and follow the track for a few yards more, then turning right along the track across the field. At the end of this cross the canal bridge and then rejoin the towpath, walking this time with the water on your right.

The Lancaster Canal

Walk alongside the canal back to the bridge beside the feed mill. Immediately before this bridge turn left, cross the stile at the end of the short track and then walk up the road to the canal bridge. Do not cross it but turn left, then left again in a matter of yards and walk along the drive to Bell Fold Farm. Walk through the unusually tidy farmyard, pass through the gate at the far end and go along the track beyond. At the end of this track go through the gate and walk across the field ahead, aiming a few yards to the right of the pylon. Cross the wide wooden bridge over the stream at the far side of this field and turn left, walking alongside New Mill Brook.

Pass by the point where some rusty pipes arch across the stream, cross into the next field and then turn right, following the hedge on your right around the edge of the field. You will eventually reach a stile beneath an oak tree; cross this and the plank bridge beyond, then walk along the right-hand edge of the field. In a short while cross a further small footbridge and then walk ahead to the end of the field just a few yards to the left of the barn and corrugated iron sheds. Climb the stile here (just behind the chevron) and turn right along the road, winding round with this, back to the pub about 300 yards away.

15. Central Lancashire: Waddington

Route: Waddington – West Bradford – Ribble Way – Grindleton – Cuttock Clough

Distance: 7 miles

Map: Explorer OL41, Forest of Bowland & Ribblesdale

Start: The Lower Buck Inn, Edisford Road, Waddington Nr Clitheroe BB7 3HU

Access: Waddington is on the B6478 road about two miles to the north of Clitheroe on the Slaidburn road. The Lower Buck Inn is just behind St Helen's church near the top of the village, not to be confused with the Upper Buck Inn in the tiny square at the top of the one long main street. Parking is very restricted both at the pub and in the village as a whole.

The Lower Buck Inn (01200 423342)

The Lower Buck Inn contributes directly to keeping the local hospital and almshouses going. Not, as in many a local pub, via collection boxes, sponsored dwyle flonking or potty hurling contests but through the rental on the property paid by licensee John Maudsley to a trust that owns the pub. The trust also supports the village hospital, hence the connection. The trust was established centuries ago by the Parker family, who still live at nearby Browsholme Hall. This powerful Lancashire family once held the title Bowbearers of the Forest of Bowland, a leading function in medieval times.

The old flag flooring is now carpeted over. The back room is the snooker room and, like the main room, simply but comfortably furnished reflecting the congenial atmosphere of this old village social centre.

The Lower Buck largely retains the atmosphere and character of the small coaching inn it once was. It was built for the Parker family, who have an interest to this day through the board of trustees; some of the roof beams in the front bar are said to be from Browsholme

The Buck (now the Lower Buck) Inn, Waddington

Hall. The original coach house survives beside the pub, and is now the residence of the licensee, John Maudsley. As befits coaching inn days there are no electronic games or musical treats.

A thoroughly traditional pub, which welcomes children. Beers served are Moorhouses Mild and Bitter, Timothy Taylor Landlord and a range of other guest beers such as Abbot Ale, Salamander and Robinsons.

Opening hours are daily from noon – 11.00pm. Home-cooked food is available Mon-Fri, noon – 2.30pm and 6.00 – 9.00pm and Sat/Sun, noon – 9.00pm.

Waddington

The village brook tumbles down through the entire length of the village, hemming in the main street which crosses and recrosses the water as and where it can, threading its way between brook side and cottage gardens which are a riot of colour for most of the year. Venerable old cottages line either side of this surprisingly wide main thoroughfare, leading up to the tiny square at the head of the village where bull baiting was once a favourite local "sport." The medieval church of St Helen's, largely rebuilt in late Victorian times, stands down a lane off the main street next to the old smithy, the village stocks and the pinfold, where stray cattle and pigs were once impounded. Across the stream is Waddington Old Hall, home to the family after whom the village is named. Henry VI took refuge here following defeat at the Battle of Hexham during the Wars of the Roses. He was informed upon however, and fled only to be captured nearby a few days later and ignominiously transported to the Tower of London tied, facing backwards, to the back of a mule. The hall can be viewed from the road but is not open to the public.

Central Lancashire

The River Ribble is the heart and soul of central Lancashire. From its source high in the Three Peaks area of North Yorkshire it sweeps in a wide swathe through the county effectively cutting it in two, separating the great northern fortress of upland Bowland from the moorland bloc of the West Pennines in the south, the northern lowlands of Amounderness from the Lancashire Plain. It is the only major river to flow westwards from the Yorkshire Dales, its source little more than a stone's throw from that of that most famous of Dales rivers, the Wharfe.

Entering Lancashire with a flourish in a deep, wooded valley near Gisburn it is throughout its length overshadowed by outlying fells – Longridge, Grindleton, Pendle Hill and Mellor Moor (all of which I include in this generous definition of central Lancashire). The steep valley sides and terraces are dappled with isolated hamlets and small villages, linked by a latticework of country lanes, tracks and greenways and virtually undisturbed by major roads. These small settlements are familiar to many – although few could name them – as they often feature in national travel and tourism guides and magazines, representative of that quintessential idyll, the English country village untouched by the passage of time.

There are only two towns of any size in the whole valley, Preston at its estuary and Clitheroe, the old Norman fortress town guarding the central Ribble Valley. These, together with Roman Ribchester and the old abbey settlement at Sawley are the only places with any river frontage to speak of. The rest is a mixture of pastureland, country estates and woodland, crossed by an occasional road but largely disturbed only by the Ribble Way footpath that is waymarked for virtually the whole length of the river. The only blot on this otherwise idyllic landscape is the cement works near Clitheroe, an infa-

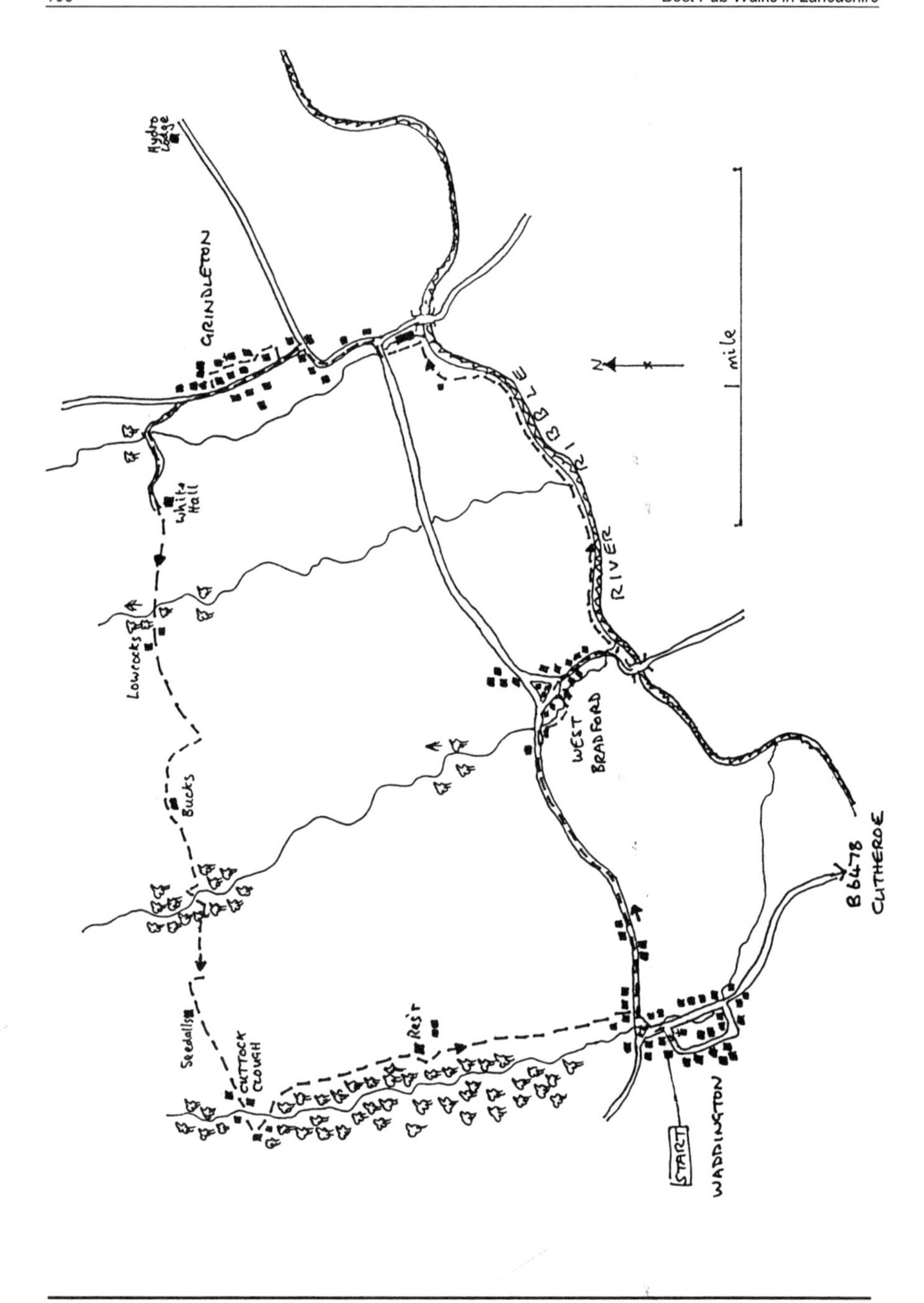

Hydro Lodge
GRINDLETON
White Hall
Lowcocks
Bucks
Seedalls
CUTTOCK CLOUGH
Rest
RIVER RIBBLE
WEST BRADFORD
N
1 mile
B6478
CLITHEROE
START
WADDINGTON

mous landmark and the only industrial intrusion of any scale in the valley upstream of Preston. This guarantees a largely unpolluted watercourse reflected in a run of salmon and sea trout matched only by the Lune in the far north of Lancashire.

There could hardly be a greater contrast to this riverscape than that other great feature of Central Lancashire, the sharp-profiled and isolated fells typified by the windswept Longridge Fell and Pendle Hill, infamous not only for its connections with witchcraft but also for sudden squalls and heavy downpours which materialise suddenly out of the clearest of skies. These outlying knuckles of Carboniferous Age sandstone and gritstone have proved more resistant to erosion than neighbouring shale deposits resulting in these local extremes of topography.

The Walk

From The Lower Buck Inn turn left, walk along past St Helen's church and down to the main street. Cross straight over both this and the stream and turn left uphill, the Sun Inn on your immediate right. At the top, turn right, you'll almost immediately see the hospital and almshouses off to your left. For the next mile, you must remain with this minor road to reach the village of West Bradford. The road is quiet, however, and furnishes good views to Pendle Hill, somewhat tarnished by the cement work chimneys.

Pass the Three Millstones pub and then turn right along the track which follows the stream down into the village – walk along with the stream on your left. At the end of this track/path, bear left past the cottage and walk along the front of the short terrace. On gaining the village street turn right and walk downhill. The old mill, now converted into luxury apartments, was in use until 1960, initially as a corn mill then a cotton mill. Continue down the hill out of the village, looking at the bottom for a public footpath sign on the left pointing towards Grindleton. Go over the stile here and join the riverside walk, a part of the Ribble Way. Remain with the riverbank and walk upstream, crossing stiles and footbridges as necessary. At one point the path leaves the river at a meander and cuts across the neck of land. Pass the small sewage works on your left here then cross the concrete bridge over the side stream, rejoining the riverbank and walking towards the long, low mill ahead.

Before you reach the mill look up to your left to spot a flight of steps and a stile beneath a large beech tree. Leave the riverbank here, climb the steps and walk along the fenced path to the road at the far end of the row of cottages. Turn right and wind uphill with the road to the village of Grindleton. Turn left up the road beside the Duke of York pub, a reminder that the village was, until 1984, in Yorkshire. You're now walking up Main Street, one of two parallel village streets. The other one, Back Lane, is off to your right and is an unmade track, worth seeking out to find the large Methodist chapel half way up. Old cottages line both of these roads that climb steeply up from the Ribble Valley.

Continue up Main Street, passing the bus turning area to reach the fork at the top of the village; bear left here, opposite Whinside House, and walk steeply downhill to the brook. On your right, you'll pass a small calcite chute formed at the outlet of a land drain. The very hard water depositing some of its load of dissolved lime in solution has formed this, in just the same way as stalactites and stalagmites form in limestone caves. Grindleton was once renowned as a minor health spa, the lime and sulphur rich waters could be taken at the Hydro Hotel to the east of the village or at Wortwells Well near White Hall. To reach White Hall just remain with the road, cross Grindleton Brook and wind uphill again. Pass the Hall on your left and walk on for a further 100 yards or so. Turn right, cross the cattle grid and then bear left at a shallow angle up the field, aiming for a stile half way along the wire fence ahead of you. Cross this, and the further stile visible ahead, walking towards the distant transmitter to cross a further stile beside two thorn trees. Once across this, walk to the far side of the field and turn left down the sunken track to the stream, crossing the footbridge here. Walk up the far side, favouring the left-hand path and cross the field at the crest of the dingle, then pass through the gate beside the new barn.

Follow the track up past the farm on your left and walk through the farmyard, leaving at the far end over the cattle grid. Remain on the surfaced drive which contours Simpsley Hill and turn right at the junction, crossing a further two cattle grids in the process. Walk up this lane, bearing left at the top to reach the gate leading to Bucks Farm. Go through the gate into the yard. The right of way actually passes behind the house and barn to reach the gate you can see at the far end of the yard, although most people tend to walk in front of the farmhouse. Go through this gate and follow the line of fence and rough track ahead. Pass through the next gate and look ahead for the gate that will lead you down into the wooded valley of Drakehouse Wood. Go through this gate, bear right and follow the path down to the stream, crossing this via the boulders and walking ahead then steeply left out of the deep cleft. At the top, look for the gate through the fence, slightly to your left. Pass through this and then bear half-right to the short, isolated section of wall, beside which is a gate. Go through this and follow the fence on your left for about 50 yards to the line of an old wall that goes up the field to your right. At this point bear half-right and walk diagonally across the field, heading for the white cottage in the distance.

Cross the cattle grid at the corner of the field and turn right up the lane, turning left at the top towards Seedalls Farm. At the end of the drive go through the gate at the sign "footpath only" and walk along the rutted track to Cuttock Clough Farm. Stay with the track through the farmyard, cross the stream and walk on up the road. Just before reaching the modern stone house on your left turn left and walk down the track with the cupressus hedge on your right. Pass the two permanent caravans and go over the little footbridge across the stream, from the far side of which walk up left to the edge of the woodland, then sticking with the woodland edge path and walking downstream. Skirt round to the right of the covered reservoir and cross directly over the track beyond. Don't go through the obvious gate but look to your right along the wall to find a high stone-step stile across the wall – it's marked by a blue hydrant sign. Once over this stile continue to follow the edge of the woods down along the long, narrow fields. Views ahead include Clitheroe, Whalley and the moors above Blackburn.

When you reach the gate at the edge of the field, at the far side of which you can see a stone barn, don't go through that gate but turn left and follow the line of fence and trees. Cross the stile beside the next gate and follow the line of trees down the field. On reaching the fence at the far side walk down the left-hand side of it and follow the line of wall, which is the hospital boundary, on your right down to the bottom. Join the road at the bottom, turn right and walk the few yards back to the top of Waddington's main street.

16. Central Lancashire: Goosnargh

Route: Goosnargh – Chingle – Longley Lane – Brook Bridge

Distance: 5.5 miles

Map: Explorer 286, Blackpool & Preston

Start: The Grapes Inn, Goosnargh PR3 2BH

Access: From Preston take the A6 north for about three miles to Broughton village crossroads (or from Junction 32 on the M6 follow the Garstang signs via Junction 1 on the M55). At the traffic lights here turn right along the B5269 towards Longridge; Goosnargh is about two miles along this road. Look for the sign on the right (just before the Stags Head) directing you left into Goosnargh village and take this, Church Lane, winding through the houses to the pub that adjoins the churchyard at the far end of the village.

The Grapes Inn (01772 865234)

The pub next to the church claims a lineage going back at least to the times of the Crusades when, for obvious reasons, it was called The Saracens Head. Landlord Hugh Gregory is confident that there was an alehouse on the site at the time of Domesday in 1086. Local legend has it that during the 15th century the incumbent parish priest at the church was also the licensee of the Saracens Head; at this time an as-yet undiscovered tunnel linking the two buildings was supposedly built. It is possible that the church silverware which disappeared after the Civil War is hidden in such a tunnel; certainly Cromwell, who used the pub as a base whilst "alterations" to the church were made, came away empty-handed. Well, almost. He had the satisfaction of renaming the pub 'The General Elliot' after one of his army commanders.

The low-beamed, multi-roomed Tetley's pub is renowned for its cask ales and offers the rambler a choice of at least six, being replaced regularly. It has been featured in the CAMRA guide for the last few years and won their "Pub of the Season" in summer 2001. There is a separate games room and the pub boasts a Crown Green bowling green, one of a large number in the area.

The Grapes Inn, Goosnargh

Harry Landless, the landlord has recently refurbished a large dining area for the serving of an extensive selection of meals. There is also a beer garden and children are welcome.

Opening hours: Mon, Tue and Wed, 11.30 – 3.00pm; Mon, 7.00 – 11.00pm; Tue and Wed, 5.30 – 11.00pm. Thu-Sat, 11.30am – 11.00pm and Sun, noon – 10.30pm. Meals are available Mon-Fri, noon – 2.30pm; Tue-Sat, 6.00 – 8.00pm and Sun, noon – 7.00pm.

Goosnargh

The name evidences the Scandinavian origins of the village; *nargh* can mean field or clearing in a wood, obviously one where geese were once penned. The history of the whole area reeks of past invaders. The land from the hills east of the village to the coast at what is now Blackpool was once known as Amounderness. Amound was King of the Vikings and the shape of the coastline in those early days was likened to that of the King's nose – Amounderness, Amound's nose. Viking ships are known to have been wrecked off the coast and analysis of old timbers in the ancient village church of St Mary the Virgin reveal that they are impregnated with sea salt and date from the 10th century, possibly timbers from wrecks on the shifting coastline just a few miles from the village.

That old triumvirate of village church, manor and pub close together is alive and well in Goosnargh. In fact there are two pubs, The Grapes and The Bushells Arms opposite, named after the Bushell family, squires of the manor, who lived in the imposing early Georgian mansion, dated 1722, which adjoins the churchyard. The last squire was Dr William Bushell. He outlived both his wife and daughter and, ahead of his time, established his mansion as a hospital for the use of "decayed gentlefolk" resident within a six-mile radius of Preston. A trust set up on his death in 1735 ensures that this stipulation remains to this day; another stipulation is that residents have four meals a day with beer at one meal and ale at another.

The village had another hospital at Whittingham Hall. This psychiatric hospital was once the second largest of its kind in Europe and totally self sufficient, with seven estate farms supplying food and materials for building and clothing; it even had its own railway line and station on a spur off the now closed Preston to Longridge line. Much of the site is now derelict, with only vestigial services being retained.

Much of Goosnargh today is modern housing to the west of the old village core, largely now a dormitory town for Preston. One building, however, predates all but the church. Chingle Hall, a small, whitewashed brick building with the remains of a moat about a mile to the south of the village, was built in 1260. It now holds claim to be the most haunted house in Britain, spectres include St John Wall, a headless martyr. There are no less than four priest holes in this, the oldest brick built domestic building still standing in Britain. The hall is open to the public daily between 10.00am and 5.00pm.

The Walk

Leaving The Grapes walk straight ahead, The Bushells Arms on your right, the mansion to the left. Where the road bends sharply left at the far end of the mansion's garden carry straight ahead along the rough track for a few yards and then turn right along the driveway leading to Bushells Cottage. Skirt the lawn on your right, the cottage to your left and walk beneath the oak tree in the rough garden beyond. Look for the stile on the right, cross this and turn left to follow

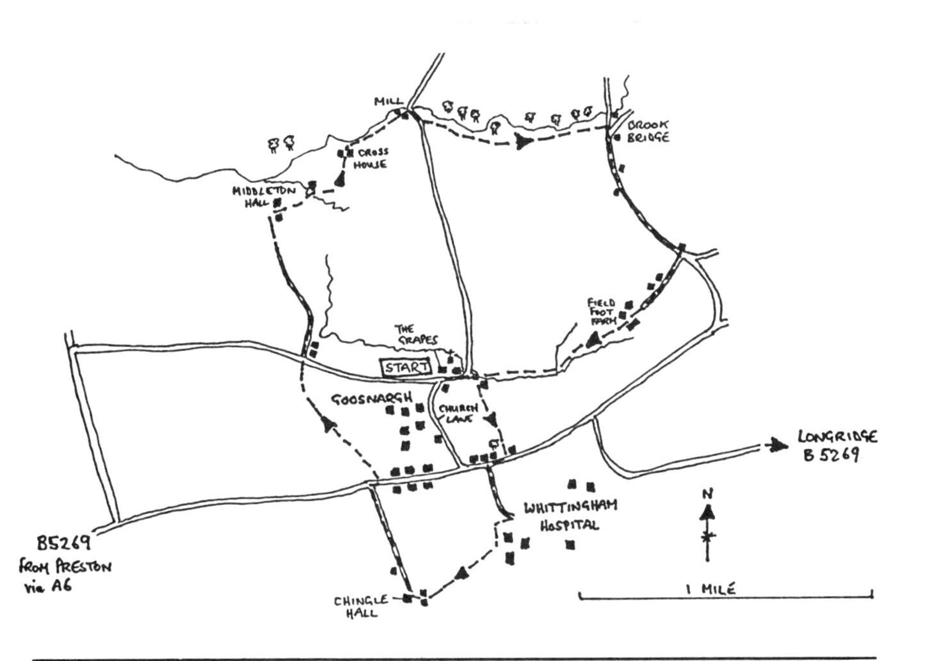

the line of hedge. Carry straight on across the field where this hedge bends left, aiming for the modern house to the left of a clump of trees at the far side of the field. These trees surround a pond; walk round the left side of this pond, cross the stile and walk up along the narrow, overgrown path up to the main road, turning right along this.

In around 100 yards, take the gate-posted driveway on the left into the grounds of the former Whittingham Hospital. Stay with this driveway for about 300 yards to find the walled Bateman House. Immediately beside the gates here, take the narrow gravelled path on your right beside the wall, soon reaching a driveway. Go over this and along the grassy path shown by a cast-iron "Footpath" sign. Pass to the right of the brick building to reach a concrete stile. Climb this and turn left, walking along to the far end of the long, low red brick barn. Remain on your side of the fence at the end and turn right following the fence, then a hedge, along two fields, crossing stiles as appropriate. A further stile takes you across a wire fence, from here head half-right to pass between the two barns (one brick, one sandstone) and turn right along the farm drive. The white building on your left here is Chingle Hall, the remains of a moat visible beside and behind the building; a short bridged causeway leads to the front entrance. Remain with the farm drive and walk to the main road at its end.

Turn right along the road and then, in less than 50 yards, take the signposted footpath off to the left, opposite a bus stop sign. Cross the stile and walk along the left edge of the field, entering the succeeding field via a stone slab stile and following the line of hedge on your right. Pass the old brick building to your left and walk along the muddy farm track to the minor road at the end. Cross directly over this and walk down the lane opposite, a directional bridleway sign indicating Longley Lane. Remain with this for about a mile. The ridge dominating the horizon ahead is the line of Bleasdale Moors, the highest point is Fair Snape Fell – at over 1600ft, one of the highest points in Lancashire; nearer to hand is the wooded knoll of Beacon Fell.

On reaching the complex of buildings that is Middleton Hall Farm, turn right to walk between a brick-pillared barn on the left and some silos on your right. The path then passes the foot of the lawn leading up to the farmhouse to reach a stile. Climb this and remain with the hedge and deep ditch to your left; where the hedge bends sharp left you should head half-left to cross a stream beneath an elm tree. Walk up the bank opposite, keeping the sparse hedge to your left, winding round at the top and following the wire fence to emerge on a farm drive beside a big new barn. Walk along the drive keeping the barn on your left then bear right into the farmyard of Cross House Farm. After only a few yards turn left and walk along with a wooden rail fence on your left and the high concrete wall surrounding the farmhouse on your right. Walk down the hill to the stream and take the stile on the right just before reaching the footbridge, skirting the bottom of the farm's garden. Cross a further stile and then follow the water for several hundred yards.

On the opposite bank, major engineering work has been undertaken to prevent bank collapse. Soon after this, on your bank, look for a stile hidden behind a large fallen tree, virtually next to the water. Climb this, follow the water for a short distance then bear right with the path into a cultivated garden passing a greenhouse to your left, sheds to your right. Ahead is the redeveloped Goosnargh Mill, on the left the mill house itself. Walk through the yard between these two buildings and along the drive to the road, turning right here to walk a short distance uphill. Where the road bends right, take the stile on the left into the field and walk ahead along the river terrace, a rough hedge to your left beyond which is the old mill leat and beyond this the stream. Cross the next stile between two thorn bushes and remain parallel to the river. The site of the old weir supplying the leat is vaguely discernible down to your left, at which point the stream arcs away left; you should remain on a straight heading and walk to the tall oak tree at the far left corner of the field.

Walk to the left of this tree, keep the hedge to your right and then leave the field via the stile at the far end. Cross the track and climb the substantial wooden stile opposite, a few yards further on the stream reappears on your left. Pass beneath the line of pylons and walk along the edge of the field towards the stone house in the distance at Brook Bridge. Climb down to the minor road and turn right along it, bearing right again at the junction to walk along Eaves Green Lane. Stay with this for the next half mile or so, passing several houses en route including the fine Brook Cottage on your left. Opposite an ivy-clad cottage, and before the road bends sharply right, turn right along the drive towards Field Foot Farm – you can't miss it as there's a large fawn-coloured sign-board.

Walk along to the farm, passing two bungalows on your right. On reaching the complex of farm buildings walk straight ahead, battery houses to both sides, silos to your left, then to your right. Enter the field at the far end and bear right, crossing through a further field gate and then turn left. Walk along the line of the hedge to your left, cross a stile and then follow the stream to a footbridge. Cross this, turn right and look for a further footbridge (simply a stone slab) about 100 yards along. Recross the stream here and turn left, following the course of the stream. At the end of the field cross the stile (about 20 yards upfield from the stream) and walk across the meadow to a further stile by a gate. Climb this, turn left and follow the driveway around to the road, from which point The Grapes is visible in the distance.

17. Central Lancashire: Holden

Route: Holden – Bolton-by-Bowland – Bolton Park – Sawley – Till House

Distance: 6 miles

Map: Explorer OL41, Forest of Bowland & Ribblesdale

Start: The Copy Nook Hotel, Holden, Bolton-by-Bowland

Access: Holden is a hamlet immediately west of Bolton-by-Bowland, about six miles north-east of Clitheroe. Join the A59 and drive towards Skipton. About three miles beyond Clitheroe (which the A59 bypasses to the south) turn left at the sign to Sawley and Bolton-by-Bowland; look for the brown road sign for Sawley Abbey. Wind through Sawley, cross the river bridge and bear right towards Bolton. The Copy Nook is a further two miles along this road, on the left at a sharp bend and junction.

The Copy Nook Hotel (01200 447205)

The Copy Nook Hotel, is a free house with a good name in the area for splendid food – a range of dishes using fresh fish and game as well as the more usual roasts. There is usually a choice of Tetley's and Marston's Pedigree bitters.

The history of the pub has been lost in the mists of time, as has the origin of its name. Until late last century it was, like many in the area, a working farm-cum-pub. It's now a small country inn and free house with a growing reputation for the quality of its food as well as its selection of beers. There's a cosy atmosphere in the open-plan bar area with log fire.

You'll find the Copy Nook closed on Mondays, but open Tue-Sun from 11.00am – 3.00pm and 6.00 – 11.00pm (for non-residents) and all day Sunday. Food (all home prepared using local produce and stock) is served each lunchtime (noon – 2.00pm) and evening (7.00 – 9.30pm) except Mondays, and all day Sunday. The choice to stay overnight is now available with six en-suite rooms.

The Walk

(*The route of this walk near Till House Farm is very ambiguous, the route recommended here is based on the evidence of home-made waymarking and of previous walkers. The walk also involves fording the river near Bolton-by-Bowland. When you enter the village note the condition of the water. If it is clear and/or low then you'll have no problem with the fording. If, however, the river is dirty and high then the ford will be impassable and you should take the alternative route outlined*).

Turn left out of the pub and left again to walk up the narrow road beside the pub towards Slaidburn. In a few hundred yards you will reach Holden itself, a huddle of cottages on the banks of the deeply incised Holden Beck. Bear left at the junction and cross the bridge over the Beck, then turn immediately left along the track and pass by the end of the old pack horse bridge. Go through the left-hand gate and walk along the pastureside above the river; down to your left is a spectacular waterfall whilst slightly upstream the water tumbles over a series of natural stone steps.

Follow Holden Beck downstream, cross the stile and remain with the river for a further 50 yards or so, then bear right and walk over to the far right-hand corner of the field, in line with the road you can see climbing a short bank. At the corner cross the stile and descend the steep steps, then follow the road right and up the hill to reach Bolton Peel Farm on your right, a fine solid old farmhouse with an old cross in front of it beside the road. Opposite the entrance to the farmyard and on your left a stone step stile takes you over the wall, thence scramble down the steep slope and walk to the footbridge over the beck. Cross this and head slightly right across the field, passing about 10 yards to the right of the telegraph pole and climbing the river terrace to the stile over the wire fence – it takes a little finding, so persevere.

Once across this walk in line of sight towards the white house on the distant hillside. Cross the next stile and then walk along the line of fence off to your left, beyond which is a pond. Beside the isolated oak tree on the ridge top is the base of an old cross, from here walk down to the corner of the field with the sheep pens and dip. Cross the stile here then walk virtually straight ahead up the long farm drive to its end, turn right and cross the bridge to walk into Bolton-by-Bowland.

Bolton-by-Bowland

Yorkshire, of which the village was a part until 1974, is famous for

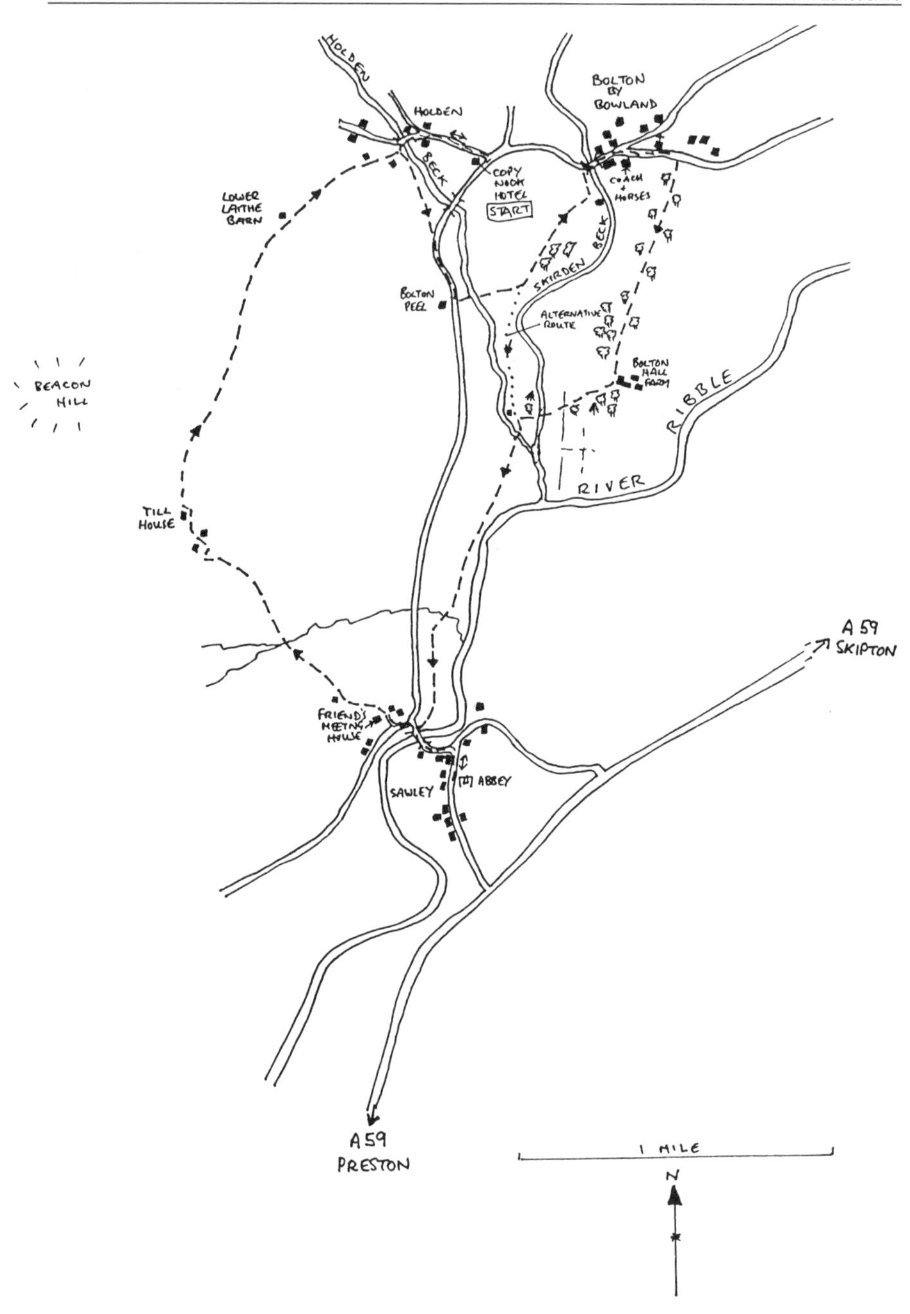
HOLDEN
HOLDEN
BOLTON BY BOWLAND
BECK
COPY NOOK HOTEL
START
COACH + HORSES
LOWER LAITHE BARN
SKIRDEN BECK
BOLTON PEEL
ALTERNATIVE ROUTE
BEACON HILL
BOLTON HALL FARM
RIBBLE
RIVER
TILL HOUSE
A 59 SKIPTON
FRIEND'S MEETING HOUSE
SAWLEY
ABBEY
A 59 PRESTON
1 MILE
N

its village greens; Bolton-by-Bowland has two of them. The lower, smaller one retains a 13th-century market cross and the village stocks and is bordered by Kirk Beck, a smattering of cottages and the village inn, The Coach and Horses (real ales and good food available). The village's one main street, lined at its western end with terraces of tiny cottages which retain mounting blocks and a solid external staircase, winds between the two greens past one of the village centre farms which remain the heart of the community.

The village church of St Peter and St Paul stands on the hillside between the two greens. It, too, dates back to the 13th century and its features include a hagioscope, or leper's squint, through which such unfortunates could watch a service, and a massive studded oak door complete with well-worn wooden sanctuary bar, used to block the door from within by those seeking sanctuary in the church. There is also a list of rectors going back to 1304; two of them gave exceptional service, William Pudsay from 1448 to 1507 and Richard Dawson from 1773 to 1826. The most impressive feature, however, is the tomb of Sir Ralph Pudsay in the chantry chapel. He had three wives and twenty five children; the relief-tomb depicts all these with the number of children each wife gave him carved in roman numerals at the feet of the appropriate wife.

Sir Ralph lived at the now-demolished Bolton Hall (it burned down earlier this century) and offered sanctuary there to Henry VI after the Battle of Hexham in 1464. It is said that the king whiled away some of his short time there in redesigning the tower of the church, the results of which may be seen today. The village's other, larger green lies to the east of the church, a massive open area bounded by buildings which include the old courthouse where guardians of the ancient Forest Laws used to decide on rights of residence in the Forest of Bowland.

If the water in the river is clear and low then leave the village along the long, tree-lined drive, opposite the church, which once led to Bolton Hall. Cross over the ridge and walk down to the white gate at the edge of the woodland, marked by a notice "Private BHE". This is the public footpath so go through the gate and wind along through the plantation to emerge in a large grass covered yard at the far end of which is a white cottage at the end of a line of barns. Turn right down the track at your side of this grassed area and pass through the gate at the bottom. From here turn right, pass to the right of the stand of trees in the field and walk ahead to the river, aiming in line of sight for the left-hand end of the line of oak and Scots pine woodland on the terrace ahead, crossing an awkward and wide drainage ditch en route. Fording the river is easy at this point, just use the lines and humps of stones and pebbles and wade through water only two or three inches deep. Once on the far bank pass to the left of the line of trees and walk left along the terrace to the footbridge.

Alternative route

If the water is dirty or higher than normal then retrace your steps from Bolton-by-Bowland, recross the river bridge and turn left down the farm drive, enter the field by the sheep pens and walk up to the base of the old cross by the oak tree. Cross the stile in the fence beyond this and then join the woodland edge on the left. Bend gradually round left with this and then walk straight across the fields ahead, crossing stiles as necessary and join the stream on your right. Pass the line of oak and pine on your left, climb the stile out of the field just beyond these trees and walk ahead along the terrace to the footbridge mentioned above.

Cross the footbridge and bear half-left to cross the stile between the two gnarled old oak trees. Walk to the far right-hand corner of the field you are now in, heading essentially for the low hilltop in the valley ahead. Cross the stile at this corner and then follow the riverbank along to the next stile. Climb this and then follow the line of white stones across the field – the path does not follow the riverbank. If it is frosty or snowing then the stones won't be obvious; your line of travel is at a shallow tangent to the right away from the riverbank which will bring you to a sleeper bridge across a stream about half way down the right-hand edge of the field. Cross this and turn left, remaining with the line of hedge on your right until you reach the bridge at Sawley. It's worthwhile making a short detour here to visit Sawley, so cross the bridge and walk along to the village, bearing sharp right at the Spread Eagle Hotel.

Sawley

A compact little village huddled beneath the steep slopes of Noddle Hill, Sawley owes its existence to William de Percy who, in 1148, endowed a Cistercian abbey on the narrow floodplain of the Ribble

Sawley Abbey

here at Salley, translated as "Land of the Willows." The founding monks came from the massive Fountains Abbey. It was an ideal spot for a Cistercian community, the White Monks were renowned for their agricultural and fish farming skills and a small but thriving community survived until the dissolution in 1536 when it was recorded as being the poorest religious House in Yorkshire (in which county it was until 1974), largely due to its proximity to the larger Whalley Abbey just a few miles away. In the following centuries the abbey buildings were severely vandalised to provide building stone for local projects – the barn by the river bridge, for example, has obviously relied on such stone – resulting in the scant remains which line the side of the village road today. The few surviving walls and arches are a shadow of its former glories, surrounding field marks and crop marks give a far better impression of the complete settlement. The abbey, to which admission is free, is closed on Mondays.

Surprisingly the village no longer has a church or chapel, although there is a Quaker meeting room across the river. There was once a calico printworks in the village but this was closed just after the Napoleonic Wars; the building then saw use as a Methodist chapel before being converted into three-storey cottages. By-passed by the busy A59, Sawley is now a tranquil backwater and a favourite stop for walkers on the Ribble Way that passes through the village.

Return to and re-cross the river bridge and go left at the junction a few yards further on. In a short while turn right up the narrow road leading up to the Friends' (Quakers') meeting house. At the end go into the driveway of Green End Cottage and walk round to the left of the garage to reach the field gate at the top of the garden, cross through this and then, as the notice suggests, follow the white markers across the fields for the next half mile or so. Some are more obvious than others and may be painted on trees or fence posts, or bottoms of white plastic containers tied to bushes or bits of old white porcelain sinks.

After about half a mile, these markers seem to disappear. The last one you will come to is in the top right-hand corner of the field after you cross a footbridge over the Sliping Brook. Once over the stile marked by this last white board stick to the left of the field and walk uphill, crossing the stile in the top left-hand corner of this field and the subsequent one a few yards further on. From here, the way is not at all obvious. I have followed the tracks left by previous walkers as a guide.

Once over the last stile bear three-quarters right to the gap in the wall and join the rough track at the corner here below the barn and farmhouse. Walk down the track for a few yards, climb the rail fence across it and then climb the bank on the left to the metal gate. Pass through this and walk across the pasture to the small barn, passing to the left of this to reach a farm driveway, then turning right up this. The right of way here passes behind the farmhouse but when I last did the walk, chalked arrows and white markers led up through the farmyard so this is the route I followed. Wind through the yard and up the drive beyond for a few yards to the point where it bends to the left. Here, straight ahead of you, rough stone steps climb the wall to a stile. Cross this stile and follow the field boundary straight ahead. At the end of this field cross the stile and walk slightly right across the shallow valley and rough pasture ahead to the further stile which is at the corner of the wire fence on the bank top ahead. Just before you reach this you cross one of the old greenways that criss-cross this area, Rodhill Lane.

Views from this point stretch across Ribblesdale to the distinctive shape of Pendle Hill and well up the meandering, wooded valley of the Ribble; to your left the start of the higher fells above Grindleton. Once over the stile walk roughly in line with the fence on your left, falling away very gently downhill to cross another stile barely 15 yards downslope from the top fence. Continue to work gently down to the break of slope and then remain at this level along the hillside. Pass above a spring marked by a holly tree and then cross through a field gate some distance ahead. At the far side of this next field, go through the gate marked by an old sink and then head for the isolated barn at Lower Laithe.

Cross the stile to the right of the barnyard and walk on to the field gate at the far side, go through this then follow the sunken track/stream down to the stile and gate. Beyond the gate walk straight ahead towards the hamlet of Holden; keep to the right of the hedge and, once past the end of this, aim to walk past the lone oak tree then down to the bottom right corner where the farm track curves away out of the field. About 15 yards to the right of the gate and cattle grid at this corner is a small stone stile at a gap in the line of holly bushes. Climb over this and walk a couple of paces to your right up the lane to the bend. Here go through the field gate on your left and walk down the field to the barn. Cross the stile in the left-hand corner and walk down the track away from the redeveloped barn. Go through the gate at the end and along to the road, turn right, cross the bridge and bear right at the junction to return to the Copy Nook.

18. Central Lancashire: Ribchester

Route: Ribchester – Stydd – Duddel Brook – Knowle Green – Buckley Gate

Distance: 8 miles

Map: Explorer 287, West Pennine Moors

Start: The White Bull, Ribchester PR3 3YP

Access: Ribchester is on the banks of the Ribble about nine miles east of Preston and four miles north of Blackburn. From Preston, take the A59 towards Clitheroe and Skipton. At the traffic lights in Clayton-le-Dale (about three miles past Samlesbury aerodrome) turn left along the B6245 signposted to Ribchester. From Blackburn take the A666 towards Whalley and Clitheroe, turning onto the B6245 (signposted to Ribchester) in Wilpshire. Park in the pay & display car park in Ribchester, walk back to the entrance to the car park road and turn right along Church Street. The White Bull is about 50 yards along on your left.

The White Bull (01254 878303)

A pub since 1707, the building was previously Ribchester's Courthouse; when the justice donned the black cap the executions were carried out in Gallows Lane, just round the corner. The grand facade is greatly enhanced by the massive porch that is supported on four stone pillars. These pillars are said to be from the Roman Temple to Minerva, which once stood some distance away; they were found in the river and recycled by the enterprising courthouse builders. Above this porch the imposing pub sign looms large, a carved wooden white bull hanging proud above the street. The pub fronts one side of the village's tiny square, other sides are hemmed in by old terraces and cottages, most of which have Roman stonemason's work incorporated into their fabric.

Inside, the pub is furnished rather like a country house hotel, comfortable seating and reserved wall decorations, largely old prints, dot the main bar area. There's a small, separate games room and a large dining area – with an excellent reputation for the quality

The White Bull

and range of food available, catering for both carnivores and vegetarians alike. One carnivore that won't be eating at the pub, however, is a fox; look ahead up the stairs as you enter the pub to catch my drift. Food is available each lunchtime and on all but Monday evenings. There's a beer garden at the back which gives extensive views up the Ribble, over to Pendle Hill and across the site of the old Roman Bath House, immediately behind the pub, an excellent location in which to enjoy the Boddingtons or one of the three guest beers on offer. The White Bull is open daily from 11.30am – 3.00pm, 6.30pm – 11.00pm, and all day on Sunday.

Ribchester

Asterix, or at least his British counterparts, would have felt at home here on the Celtic fringe of the Roman Empire. The Romans took over the site of a Bronze-Age settlement and, in about AD70, established a major fort and outpost that they named Bremetennacum Veteranorum on the road from (present day) Manchester to Lancaster. Largely garrisoned first by Spanish and then Hungarian cavalry troops – subjects of the Empire rather than Romans *per se* – the fort survived until the Romans withdrew from the north in the 4th century. Patterns of trade developed and the invaders intermingled with the local Brigantes tribe, remaining in the area after the collapse of the Roman Empire.

Much of the fort has either been washed away by the changing course of the Ribble or is buried beneath the 13th-century St Wilfred's church and churchyard, but you can visit the old granaries and the bath house. The Temple to Minerva, source of the White Bull's columns, is thought to have been at or near the site of the present church; the columns were recovered from the Ribble at this point. An excellent museum near the church details the Roman history of the town; exhibits include a copy of the best-preserved ceremonial helmet ever found in Britain, inevitably the original is in London's British Museum. The Museum in Ribchester is open daily from 9am and on Saturday & Sunday afternoons only (01254 878261).

Town is perhaps too grand a word to apply to the pleasant large village that exists today. A few streets of long, low, gritstone and sandstone cottages cluster round Church Street and Water Street, meeting at the tiny square outside The White Bull and interlinked by winding ginnels. More modern development lingers on the fringes beyond the Blackburn road and the village's other Bull pub, The Black Bull.

Most of the industry – largely weaving – has long since died out to leave the village as a peaceful backwater. The Roman ford (or bridge if there ever was one) has long gone and the main road now skirts the village to a "new" bridging point a mile or so upstream. Just off this road the tiny hamlet of Stydd has a remarkable old chapel, dating back to the 1100's, that once belonged to the Order of the Knight's Hospitallers of St John, one of only a handful of chapels dedicated to this order (based in Jerusalem) in Britain. It is kept locked and is rarely used but the low leaded windows allow a view of the austere stone-flagged, whitewashed, stone and wooden interior.

The Walk

Turn right from The White Bull and walk along Water Street for about 50 yards, then turn right again along Greenside, winding with this to its end and passing the route to the Bath House on the way. At the end turn right along the main Blackburn Road. Pass the Ribchester Arms on your left and walk along to reach Stydd Lane on the left, immediately before the bridge over the stream. Turn up this lane and follow it to its end. You pass the small church of St Peter and St Paul off to your left and, nearer to hand, the small but grandiose almshouses dating from 1726. Go through the farm gate at the end and walk up the drive beyond to Stydd Chapel, set in its own pastureland to your right. Remain with the track and walk up through the farmyard of Stydd Manor. At the far end leave the yard by the stile to the right of the farm gate and simply follow the rough field track up the long field beyond.

At the top right-hand corner of this field are two gates. Cross the stile to the far right and bear right, passing around the top of a rough hollow and walk towards the woodland ahead, aiming for the tallest trees. Join a hedge on your right and follow this to a small enclosure of trees. Immediately to the left of this are two stiles close together; cross these and continue towards the woods. Access into these woods is gained by the stile about 70 yards up from the corner; once in the woods walk down the path beyond to the stream, Duddel Brook. Cross the footbridge here, walk ahead for a few yards and then turn left along the path which parallels the stream down to your left in its deep, almost gorge like valley. In a short while you will reach the tumbled remains of Duddel Brook (or Dutton) Mill, an old comb mill (combs for use in the woollen industry, not hair care). It is worth spending a little time exploring these remains in this spectacular setting – including the mill leat and weir upstream – before descending to the footbridges, both of which you now cross.

From the end of the second bridge, follow the path gradually up the valley side to its crest. There is a stile on your left behind an oak tree. Ignore this, and the path ahead, instead favouring the narrow path that goes steeply downhill to reach the stream; in places you'll have to scramble down rock outcrops and over fallen rocks and tree roots. You reach the stream at a very picturesque spot; to your left Duddel Brook tumbles over a waterfall into an amphitheatre-like glade whilst ahead a small brook torrents down to the main stream. Here you should ford Duddel Brook – there are plenty of stepping stones – and climb up the valley side opposite, bisecting the angle between the main stream and the brook. On reaching the wire fence at the top walk left to reach a stile beneath the second oak tree and cross into the field. Turn left and follow the woodland edge along to a further stile. Cross this and head half-right across the field, head-

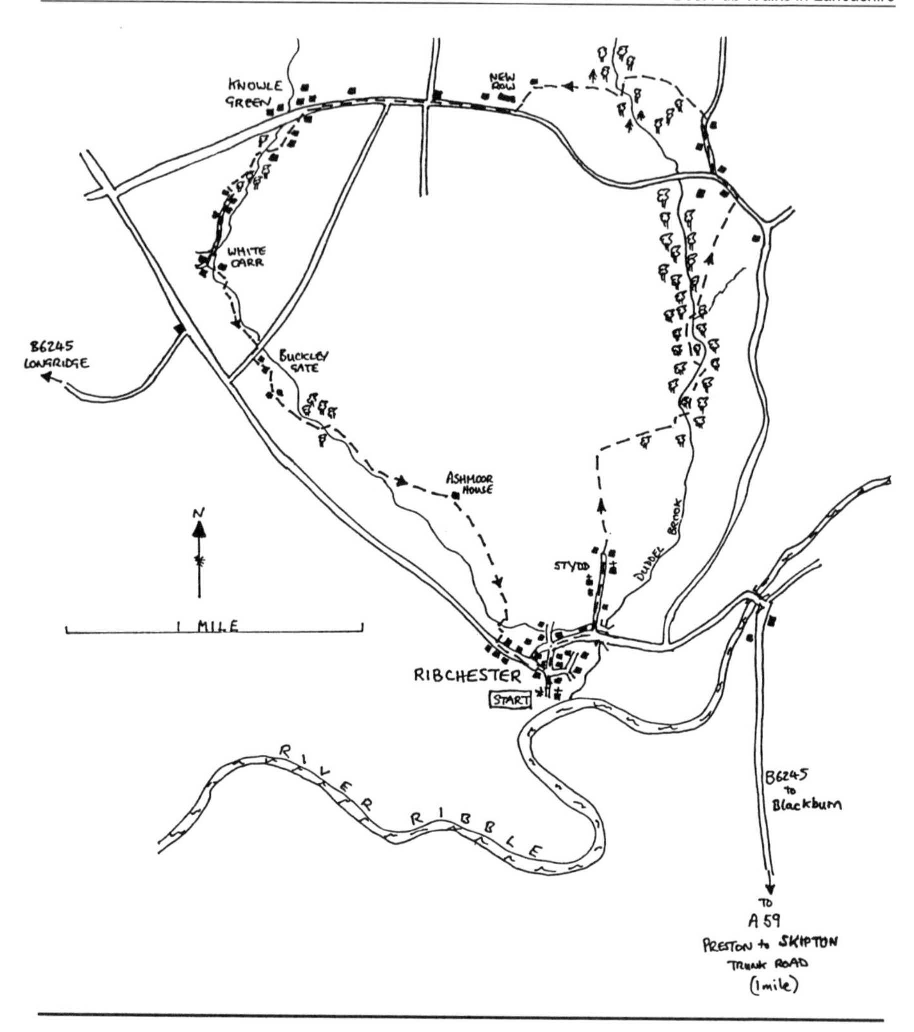

ing for the field gate at the middle of the long hedge you are walking towards. The stile out of the field is to the right of this gate, cross it and turn left along the road.

At the junction turn right up Huntington Hall Lane and follow this for about 400 yards, passing the white cottage on your right. At the sharp bend beyond this go through the kissing gate and then head for the caravan you will see a few hundred yards ahead. Go through the gate here, pass to the right of the caravan – Dingle Dell –

and walk to the end of the paddock, just past the ruined wire enclosure. Climb the stile here and turn half-left, walking now to the line of the woods at the far side of the field. Head for the tallest tree you can see, the stile into the woods is below this and leads to a path beneath a bower of rhododendron bushes. Follow this path to the driveway and turn left; cross the bridge and then take the path immediately to the right up to the kissing gate. Pass through this and then follow the woodland edge, part of the large estate of Dutton Manor, on your right.

Where the woods end continue along the fence to the corner, cross the stile and walk to the barn about 200 yards away. Go over the stile into the yard and then down the muddy track beyond, following this to its end just past the row of cottages, New Row. Turn right along the main road here and remain with it for nearly a mile, passing en route the Halls Arms at a crossroads marking the route of the old Roman road from Ribchester to Lancaster.

On reaching the hamlet of Knowle Green, look on your left for the tiny Congregational church and adjoining manse. A few yards downhill a driveway leads off to the left, walk along to the end of this, bearing right as necessary, to reach Clay Cottage. The drive passes to the right of the cottage and garden to end suddenly. To the right at this point descend the steep, railed steps that pass by an ivy-covered ruined mill to the footbridge. Cross this bridge and bear left with the path, following it along the woodland edge. On reaching the tall stile look down to the left and climb down the slippery steps to the old barn, continuing beyond this to join the narrow road, then following this along with the stream down to your left.

On reaching the ford, take the path off to the right, cross the footbridge and walk along to another ford on your left. Ahead is a footbridge, cross this and walk straight ahead passing between the rebuilt hall on your right and the renovated cottage to your left, White Carr. Enter the field ahead and walk down to the footbridge about 50 yards away. Cross this, turn left and follow the brook downstream to emerge on a narrow road about a quarter of a mile on. Turn right here then left down the drive within 50 yards to pass in front of a cottage and adjoining chicken sheds. Walk to the end of the drive and pass to the left of the house, the former Buckley Mill. At the corner here, below the chimney a footbridge comes in from the left. Do not cross this but turn right, pass through the mill yard and walk across the lawn to the stile over the fence. Climb this and walk diagonally up the field beyond, climbing a further stile and then aiming for the small black cattle shed you can now see. Cross the stile to the right of this and turn left along the drive into the farmyard of Buckley Hall.

Pass straight through the farmyard, leaving by the gate beside the small barn and then walk half-left across and down the pasture, aiming for the far left-hand corner marked by the gaunt skeleton of a large dead tree. Cross the stile on the left near this tree and walk down the steep slope to the footbridge. On your left, the fenced-off area marks the top of an old, capped, mineshaft; inspection of the riverbank below reveals evidence of shaley coal deposits. Cross the footbridge and walk ahead alongside the river. At the end of the field cross the footbridge over the side stream, about 20 yards off the main river. Once across walk half-left up the slope, passing through the obvious gaps in two old hedges. At the top bear right and walk to the isolated Ashmoor House. The path passes in front of the house, so enter the garden via the wooden fence next to the gate at the side of the house and walk along in front of the house to the drive. Remain with this, crossing two cattle grids. Some 20 yards before the next cattle grid, bounded by two stone gateposts, turn to the right. A line of stiles aligned with the chimney in Ribchester will bring you to a funnel-ended field. Here, cross the wide concrete bridge, bear half-left to a stile, cross this and turn right along the track which runs beside the site of an engineering works. At the end turn left along the road and walk back into the village centre.

19. Rossendale: Cowpe

Route: Cowpe – Cowpe Lowe – Dearden Clough – Scout Moor – Rossendale Way – Boarsgreave

Distance: 8.5 miles

Maps: Explorer OL21, South Pennines

Start: The Buck Inn, Cowpe BB4 7DR

Access: From Rawtenstall take the A681 road eastwards towards Bacup. In Waterfoot bear right at the traffic lights by The Railway pub and continue along Bacup Road for about 100 yards. On the right, immediately past Barclays Bank, is the narrow Cowpe Lane – there's a picnic site signpost pointing up the road. Go up Cowpe Lane and wind around with it, pass the picnic site entrance on your right and then look for the Buck's car park on the left. The pub itself is a few yards further up the road.

The Buck Inn (01706 213612)

Cowpe Brook has cut a deep, sinuous clough into the high gritstone moors immediately south of the great trough cut by the Irwell, of which the Cowpe is a tributary. The one narrow road winds up the valley to the surviving mill at the end, lined by dark gritstone terraces, the tumbled remains of long gone mills and old lodges, hemmed in all round by the sombre moorland tops. Hardly the sort of place you'd expect to find a convivial local such as The Buck. Yet the pub survives – just – as very much of a "local's local" as the saying goes, at the same time offering a haven and a welcome for the increasing number of ramblers who are discovering this area.

I say "just" surviving as the pub is not open on Monday to Thursday lunchtimes; landlady Doreen Williams found it uneconomical. However, Friday and Saturday lunchtimes (noon – 3.00pm), each evening (7.00 – 11.00pm) and all day Sunday, finds the stack of pumps on the bar busy dispensing Tetley's Smooth and John Smiths Smooth, Jenning's Bitter and Green's Bitter. The pub is, essentially two houses at the end of one of the terraces about half way up the valley. There's one large main room with an area set aside for pool and other pub games. The rest of the room is crowded with tables, stools and wall seats, warmed in the winter by a fire in the solid, gritstone fireplace. A stag's (buck's) head stares sightlessly from his spot above this fireplace, sharing the walls with a great variety of brasses, prints, keys, spoons, lamps and similar artefacts; brass/copper kettles and scuttles adorn the fireplace. The Buck is a great place to unwind after a long circuit of the moors; bar meals are available at weekends and children are made welcome.

Rossendale

Rossendale derives its name from the old Forest of Rossendale, a royal hunting demesne established for the pleasure of the Norman and Plantagenet monarchs of centuries ago. There can have been few trees even then, the acid soils and steep cloughs conspiring to ensure that the moorland heights remained the preserve of red deer and wolves, both long since gone, together with hares and rabbits to entertain the royal whim for falconry.

Present-day Rossendale incorporates the Forest of Rossendale to the north of, and a swathe of high moorlands to the south of, the River Irwell. The river rises in the forest, flows via Rawtenstall, Bury and the outskirts of Bolton to Salford, from where it is canalised as the Manchester Ship Canal. The Irwell's narrow valley floor is virtually infilled by high concentrations of terraced houses, mills and related industries, interspersed by areas of woodland and open spaces reclaimed from derelict mill sites. The local Groundwork Trust, one of the first to be established, has made great strides in this direction and the local authorities are doing their bit by way of establishing a regional footpath, The Irwell Valley Way. This complements the well-established Rossendale Way that offers a high level circuit of the Borough of Rossendale; the route runs from the river's source above Bacup to Salford, and incorporates a Sculpture Trail.

In centuries past this high moorland provided rich pickings for quarrymen – the area is littered with workings large and small, almost all long-abandoned to nature. Old packhorse and coach routes criss-cross the tops, sunken tracks and footpaths interlinking with these in a devilishly complex web. The deep cloughs were host to countless mills; old leats, ponds and ruins abound but few remain working today.

The most inspiring remains, however, are the trackbeds of the old tramways and ephemeral railways that served the quarries together with the slab-paved roadways which once saw horse drawn wagons or sleds transporting heroic-sized lumps of rock to the cutting and dressing shops and to the valley below. The best time to visit the tops is on a crisp, bright winter's day, frost decorating the sedges and mosses and with the low sun and a dusting of snow picking out these man-made artefacts to a tee.

The Walk

Leave The Buck and walk downhill to the end of the terrace, then branch left and walk along in front of Brookland Terrace. At the far end of this turn left and walk up the rough road between the green garages, starting a steep climb up the side of the valley. Remain with this road and wind round to reach the house at the top. Go through the gate to the right of this renovated house and barn and immediately look for the stone trough to the right, beside which is a stile you should climb. Once over it stick with the field boundary on your left and walk up through the rough pastures, crossing stiles as and when necessary.

Pass by the fence made largely of corrugated iron sheeting and continue straight up the hillside to the moorland track, turning right along this. Ahead of you the flat-topped hill is Cowpe Lowe, to your right a wide prospect over the Rossendale Valley to Bacup and, beyond here, the high moorlands on the West Yorkshire boundary, the edge of Brontë country. Walk on around the end of the hill, Black Hill, passing a deep, sharp cleft cut into the side of Cowpe Lowe on your right. Cross the stile to the left of the gate, walk straight across the track which is evidently heavily used by scrambling bikes and then bear half-right, aiming for the gap in the embankment ahead. This embankment is the line of one of the old tramways which led from Cragg Quarry; your route lies along it so when you get to the gap scramble up onto the bank and walk with it off to the right along and around the southern flank of Cowpe Lowe.

Remain with this tramway for about a quarter of a mile; it eventually merges with the line of an old cartway across the moor, the rutted and worn slabs still standing proud along the route. Views ahead extend to Peel's Monument above Ramsbottom. At the point where a deep-walled trench appears on your left you should bear left over the short bank across this and then walk along the track known as Sand Beds Lane. Glimpses into the Irwell Valley are allowed here, the large cream area on the far hillside to your right is an artificial ski

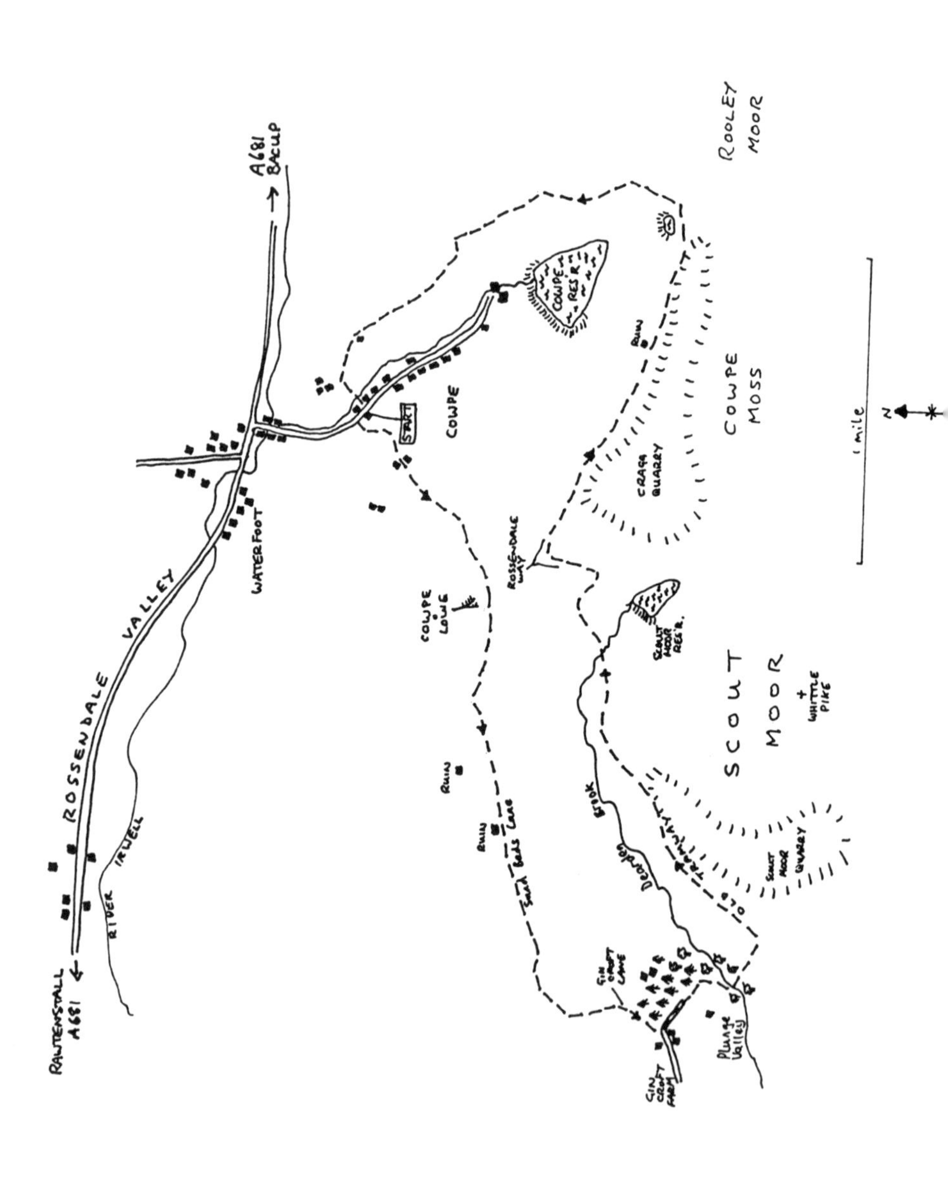
ROSSENDALE VALLEY
RAWTENSTALL A681
A681 BACUP
RIVER IRWELL
WATERFOOT
START
COWPE
COWPE LOWE
COWPE RES'R
ROOLEY MOOR
COWPE MOSS
CRAGG QUARRY
ROSSENDALE WAY
RUIN
SCOUT MOOR
SCOUT MOOR RES'R
WHITTLE PIKE
SCOUT MOOR QUARRY
Dearden Brook
GIN CROFT LANE
GIN CROFT FARM
Plunge Valley
1 mile
N

slope above Rawtenstall. Cross the high stile when you reach it and remain with Sand Beds Lane. Several ruined farms are passed including the eponymous Sand Beds; it is impossible to imagine what life was like for the Victorian farmer in this wild, inhospitable place.

At the gate, climb the ladder stile and walk along the track between the high banks, turning left at the end down the slightly better surfaced Gin Croft Lane. Walk down this to the junction at the end of the woods and just above Gin Croft Farm. Turn left along the tarmac road at this point and walk along, continuing straight ahead as the tarred road swings left. Wind down this increasingly sunken pathway to reach the stream at the bottom, an area known as Plunge Valley. An information board here outlines the history of the area and the fulling mill, the remains of which are a few yards downstream.

Spend a little time exploring this site before crossing the footbridge across Dearden Brook and climbing the stile, then to walk ahead up the hillside past the lone ash tree. Once at the valley crest, aim to walk ahead to pass the left end of the truncated wall. From here, to the corner of the walls pointing towards you from higher up the hillside. At this corner is a small wooden gateway giving access to the sedge-covered track on the far side. This is the line of an old tramway descending from the quarries high up the valley and you remain with the line of this for the next mile or so. The route is obvious if boggy in places but on occasion the trackbed disappears completely; simply sight it ahead and remain on the line. Old wooden sleepers remain in situ and at one point, the track is still there showing the gauge to have been about 3'6". Down to your left, the Dearden Brook has cut a glorious winding clough deep into the edge of Scout Moor. You'll have to cross several side cloughs, marked by waterfalls and on one occasion a rickety old sleeper bridge – cross just upstream as it is very slippery and precarious.

Pass through the gap in the wall marked by two old wooden gateposts and walk ahead around the hillside track, the dam of Scout Moor Reservoir coming into view ahead. Look down left into the clough to find the circular drain issuing from the hillside, just below the second cloughside wall up this deep side valley. Walk down the steep clough side to this drain and then up the equally steep far side, following the line of the wall. At the top you will come to a concreted road, a service road for the reservoir. Turn left along this, go around the hairpin bend and walk along for a further 100 yards or so, then cut left up alongside the fin-like section of wall that marks the near hillside. Walk along this, and the line of wall beyond, up the hillside to regain the concrete road again, turning left along this.

At the point where this roadway sweeps off and down to the left look for the Rossendale Way (RW) waymark on the post to your right and go along the track here, the wall on your left. In a short distance, turn right up the track and swing right with this at the ridge top, walking up towards the old quarry workings. Keep the wall close to your left, drifting away with this as it diverges left away from the main track. It's a rather melancholy landscape hereabouts, with overgrown spoil tips, chasms, sheep tracks and clumps of bilberry replacing the once thriving quarry workings here on Cowpe Moss.

Stick with the line of the wall going slowly downhill. Down on your left is the stretched polygonal lake of Cowpe Reservoir, below this is the mill at the head of Cowpe Village. Go through the rusty old gate by the standing stones and walk along to the ruin, after which the track gradually regains height. Pass through the gate you reach and walk ahead, again with the wall on your left. Cross above the small header reservoir – Cragg High Level Tank – and join the track that comes down from the right. In 100 yards or so go left at the fork and walk downhill with the descending track, remaining with this past several water board signs to the point where it joins a further track coming down from the right; on the left is a small walled quarry with a pool filling its deepest recesses.

This new track, along which you turn left, is Rooley Moor Road, an old coach road between Rochdale and Rawtenstall. Until at least the 1920s, an old coaching inn, The Moorcock, remained open about a mile to the south (behind you) on this bleak road. Walk downhill until you reach a gate across the road, then turn left and walk down alongside the brook to the gate. Go through the narrow kissing gate to the right of this and turn right, following the line of wall and ignoring the further stile on the right in a matter of a few yards. At the end of the field, go through the gate and over the stile and walk down to the isolated cottage. Pass immediately to the right of the cottage and then walk along the fence away from it to the gate at the end. From here head for the black-painted end gable of the terrace ahead. Cross the double stile before you reach this terrace and walk down the line of the vaccary slab fence, heading for The Buck which you can see in the valley below.

Vaccary fencing, Cowpe

20. Rossendale: Nangreaves

Route: Nangreaves – Walmersley – Deeply Vale – Harden Moor – Grants Tower

Distance: 7.5 miles

Map: Explorer OL21, South Pennines

Start: The Lord Raglan, Nangreaves, Bury BL9 6SP

Access: Travel north from Bury along the A56 for about two miles. On reaching the traffic lights at Walmersley Post Office (on your right) turn right up Walmersley Old Road and follow it to its end, crossing over the M66 en route. Nangreaves and the Lord Raglan are both signposted from Old Road; the last half-mile is cobbled.

The Lord Raglan (0161 764 6680)

At the top end of the hamlet of Nangreaves, The Lord Raglan is in an enviable position on the lip of one of the ridges of high moorland which reach like the fingers of a giant hand down towards Manchester. Sitting on the terrace and supping some of the excellently kept home-brewed beers (there is a thriving micro-brewery in the cellar – tours by arrangement), the immense view to the west encompasses the famous Peel's Tower on Holcombe (Harcles) Hill and the distant Winter Hill above Bolton, topped by its giant transmitter masts. Despite its proximity the M66 motorway is well screened; you're much more likely to hear the throaty cough of a steam locomotive on the East Lancashire Railway, far below, as it threads its way along the Irwell valley between Bury and Rawtenstall.

The pub is named in honour of Lord Raglan, overall commander of the British forces in the Crimean War. A clipping from the Bury Times, displayed at one end of the bar, records the death of this military man in 1855. The pub itself is somewhat older, being nearer 200 years old. Until the turn of this century it also acted as the village butchers shop and greengrocers and had its own brewhouse, the latter now being incorporated into the fabric of this large, comfortable building. The current landlord, Brendan Leyden, was born in the pub; the latest of several generations to run the business he's always on the lookout for antiques to add to the already impressive collection on display in the multi-roomed pub.

A restaurant is an integral part of the pub offering a good choice of home cooked dishes including slow-cooked shoulder of lamb. Those with less capacious appetites can choose from a wide variety of bar snacks and there's always at least one vegetarian choice on the menu. Children are welcome and muddy boots are a regular part of the scenery in this well run and welcoming pub. The Lord Raglan is open daily from noon – 2.30pm (last orders for food 2.00pm) and 7.00 – 11.00pm (last orders for food 10-ish), and all day Sunday.

Nangreaves

Apart from a few isolated farmsteads Nangreaves did not exist until the end of the 18th century when John Hall built a mill high on this hillside to the east of Ramsbottom. From 1803 until the 1960s the mill workers produced high quality cotton goods. They were housed in solid gritstone terraces adjoining the mill and enclosing the mill yard and millpond. The decline of the cotton industry in the 1960s led to the replacement of cotton as the product by polystyrene goods and this business survived until the mid 1980s when the mill was finally closed. The low mill buildings have been adapted and converted into cottages and the mill yard and pond have become a village green. The whole is now a conservation area; it is doubtful whether contemporary mill workers could afford to live in Nangreaves today.

To the north of the hamlet are the scant remains of Grants Tower. This was built in 1829 for William and Daniel Grant who first developed the calico printing industry in nearby Ramsbottom and became great benefactors to the area. It is believed that Charles Dickens modelled the Cheeryble Brothers, in Nicholas Nickleby, on the Grants. A walking guide from the 1920s records that the key to the tower was held at the nearby farm, and that panoramic views were available from the top. Sadly, only the barest of skeletons of this old tower now survives.

The Cheesden Valley

Long before the towns of south Lancashire became famous for their textile and cotton industries this tiny Pennine valley was a hive of activity, host to a dozen or more mills, dyeing and print works. They developed here to take advantage of the abundant clean water supply, local wool and emergent coal seams; only later did they partially adapt to and utilise the cheap imported cotton which eventually saw the rise of the familiar cotton towns and the decline of the industry in Cheesden – only one bleach works now remains operational, some miles downstream from this walk. The most extensive remains are those at Deeply Vale Print Works where cobbled lanes, bridges, conduits and wheel pits remain below the dam of the mill reservoir. The most spectacular remains, however, are at the very head of the valley where the façade of the Cheesden Lumb Woollen Mill all but fills the valley, brooding over the tumbled remains of countless buildings and mill lodges (ponds). The whole valley and tributaries have been recognised as a site of major historic significance by English Heritage and are under its protection.

The Walk

Turn left from the pub and walk uphill. In about 50 yards, you will find some stone steps set into the wall on your right, before you get to the farm. Climb these into the field and follow the path uphill to a stile in the corner. This short climb has opened up extensive views to the south over the Greater Manchester conurbation – city centre Manchester is easily picked out by its concentration of tall buildings – and to the Mersey estuary and the Cheshire Plain. The walk now gently descends this southern slope of Snape Hill; head towards Whitewall Farm, crossing another stone stile in the first wall you reach and then aiming for a stile directly behind the electricity pylon, about 30 yards to the right of the farm. Cross directly over the drive here and enter the field opposite, cross a further stile to the right of the small area of trees ahead and walk down to the minor road.

On reaching this road, a driveway, turn sharp left and walk down to the ivy-clad cottage. A yellow waymarker points the way from here which is down the walled path in front of the cottage and, having crossed the stile at the end, bear right. You're now in a beautiful secluded valley, well wooded with alder, sycamore, willow, thorn and oak and dotted with a string of small ponds that, long ago, provided power to the long-gone mill further down the valley. Keep half an eye out here for heron, coot, moorhen and the vivid flash of a

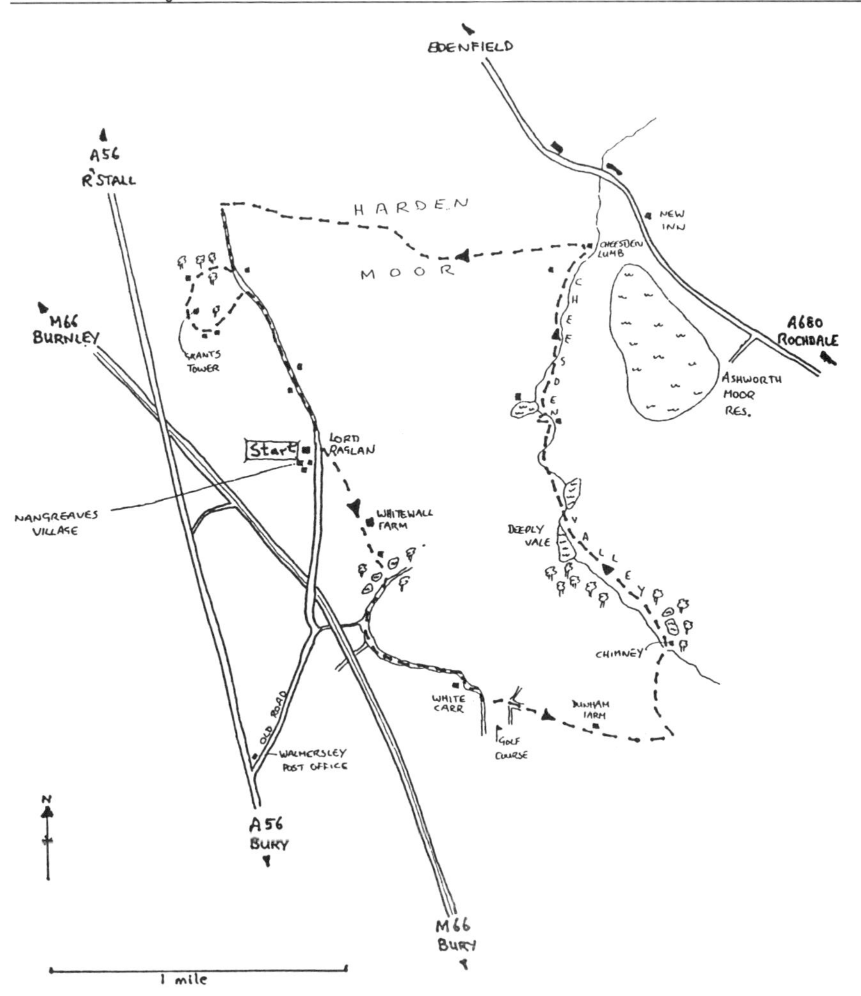

kingfisher. Cross the footbridge that forms part of one of the dam walls and scramble up the bank opposite, climbing the steep stile at the top to gain a narrow road, turning right down this. The steep bank to your left is thickly clad with bilberry plants and heather, a sure sign of approaching moorland. Ahead the M66 strides across the small valley en route from Bury to Rawtenstall whilst on your right is a flat, scrubby area and a couple of gateposts, all that remain of the mill once fed from the ponds upstream.

Before reaching the motorway bridge, the way is left, up along White Carr Lane and towards Walmersley Golf Course. Bear left again and follow this road for nearly a mile. The only building you pass is White Carr Farm, an old, low gritstone building with glorious mullioned windows. Not far past this, around the sharp bends, is a board welcoming you to Walmersley Golf Course, stretching away from you along the hillside. At this point take the stile on your left and follow the wall up the hillside, bearing right at the top to reach a gate and a signpost. Of the three possible ways, you want the middle one, signposted to Birtle Dean. This is known as Scotland Lane, a long established moorland road still, in places, surfaced with setts. Follow this road through the isolated farmyard of Dunham Farm and continue along the hillside, the deep trough of Cheesden Brook emerging ahead, the flat-topped Knowle Hill dominating the horizon.

Cross between the old stone gateposts and follow the track around the hillside for about 50 yards until a vista of the deep valley opens before you. Pause here to appreciate the view across Rochdale in the middle distance to the heights of the South Pennines at Saddleworth Moor, marked by a radio mast that also marks the route of the Pennine Way National Footpath. Down and off to your left an old chimney stack rises above the trees that cover the floor of the Cheesden Valley here, this chimney is our next target.

Turn back-left on yourself and follow the path down the steep valley side, crossing the stile at the bottom and winding across an area of old coal workings, heading always for the old chimney stack. Cross the brook by the old single-arched packhorse bridge and turn left up the valley. The chimney marks the site of the old Lower Wheel Print Works, other remains include piles of dressed stone in the swiftly flowing, crystal clear brook and some mill lodges behind the chimney. These are home, in season, to an abundance of dragonfly and damselfly, frogs, heron and various species of duck. The valley is rich, too, in mammal life, fox, rabbit, stoat, weasel and white hares can all be seen. Follow the path away from the old works and up the hillside, turning left where it joins a wider track and walk up to the woods on your left. These hide the remains of Deeply Vale Print Works, well worth exploring in detail if with a little caution.

Pass the lake on your left, at the end of which is a small quarry from whence came the stone to build the mills and construct the dams. Continue along the track, another lake appearing to your right. At the top of the slope, look ahead for the squat pylon and, beyond this, a cottage next to a waterfall. Head across the fields towards this cottage, turn left along its drive and walk along for about 100 yards, passing a large barn on your right built on the remains of Longland Cotton Mill. Once past the barn turn back-right on yourself and walk along the top of the dam. The old Buckhurst school looms over the far bank of the lake whilst beyond is the edifice of Peel's Tower. Pass through the gateposts at the end of the dam and then turn left by the telegraph pole, walk down to the stream side and follow this upstream. The way is rather indistinct for the next half mile or so and can be quite marshy beneath the veneer of sedges, reeds and mosses. Aim for the stile by the white-painted "sheep grazing" sign and work your way from here to the left of the valley floor.

Continue up the valley passing by and through overgrown old buildings and drained lodges until you reach the façade of Cheesden Lumb Woollen Mill, the last works in the valley; its splendour has recently been tempered by storm damage although work is in hand to restore this. The crenellated wall on the valley crest to the right marks the dam wall of Ashworth Moor Reservoir.

From the woollen mill, turn left immediately this side of the footbridge, pass through the stile and turn left, walking up the short moorland track to a driveway. Go straight across this and enter the field to the left of the wall, following the wall up and onto Harden Moor. The right of way across the moors here is undefined, the simplest way of remaining on course is to aim straight for Peel's Tower, visible in the middle distance. After about a mile and a half bear slightly right to head for the light coloured waste tip that marks the edge of an old quarry. Pass over several broken walls to reach the base of the spoil heap at a gate, leave the field here and turn left along Bury Old Road, an unmade, walled, moorland track. Up to the right, a large circle of stones marks the site of an old cairn on the nearby hilltop.

Take the second turn on the right, a road signposted to Hillside Kennels and graced by a sign-board in the likeness of Peter Pan. Follow the road round through the trees and into the yard of Pike Farm, then turn left and walk up the road to the small transmission station near the hilltop, passing to the right of this. Immediately beyond is the stump that is all that remains of Grants Tower; its height or view from the top can only be imagined. Follow the path around the south side of the hill (i.e. the opposite side to that which you approached it from) and walk down to the left-hand farm in the lee of the slope. Turn left here at the iron gates and follow this driveway back along to Bury Old Road, turning right along here to return to The Lord Raglan about half a mile away.

21. Rossendale: Mereclough

Route: Mereclough – Hurstwood – Swinden Valley – Worsthorne – Hurstwood

Distance: 7 miles

Map: Explorer OL21, South Pennines

Start: The Kettledrum Inn, Mereclough, Burnley BB10 4RJ

Access: The Kettledrum Inn stands beside a minor road leading from Burnley to Hebden Bridge just over two miles south-east of Burnley. From Burnley, take the A671 road past the entrance to Towneley Hall and Park and then turn onto the A646 towards Holme Chapel and Todmorden. Cross under the railway line and, on entering the hamlet of Walk Mill, turn sharp left along Park Road. After a few yards hairpin to the right and follow the road up to the T-junction in Over Town. Turn left here and remain with this road to reach Mereclough in about half a mile. The Kettledrum is the second pub on the right.

The Kettledrum Inn (01282 424591)

It's worth making the trip simply for the view from the pub, high on a ridge overlooking Burnley far below and across to Pendle Hill and the high fells of the Forest of Bowland in north Lancashire. Inside, the pub is an Aladdin's cave with brass and copper plates, weights, measures, bedpans, gauges, oil lamp bases and brass trays from long-defunct breweries. What doesn't gleam can be buffed or polished – Toby jugs, walking sticks, spears, swords, cutlasses and daggers with and without scabbards, boomerangs and hurling sticks, shuttles and shillelagh. There's a fine display of old photographs – note the one of the pub in the late 1970s to see how much work the current owners have put in – whilst upstairs in the gas-lit restaurant is an Indenture document, a deed of sale from 1825 recording the transfer of the property to a schoolmaster.

It was not until 1861 that the building became a pub, named after the Derby winner of that year which was owned by the Towneley family, Lords of the Manor, whose stately home is now a museum

The Kettledrum Inn, Mereclough

outside Burnley. The year 1861 marked an upturn in their fortunes; since then family members (including a current one) have often been High Sheriff of Lancashire. The pub once belonged to a local brewery, Masseys of Burnley, now long defunct. Nowadays it is a Pubmaster house, selling Marston's and Tetley beers on handpump (and a different guest beer each month), at the – you've guessed it – sheet-coppered bar.

Also available is a very extensive range of bar meals including a vegetarian option. Food is available from noon – 2.30pm and 6.30 – 9.00pm (Sunday noon – 7.00pm), the pub itself is open from 11.00am – 3.00pm and 5.30 – 11.00pm. Local ramblers often frequent this ideally situated pub. During the summer months, the pub is open all day.

The Walk

Leave the pub and turn left down the minor road which runs down beside it, signposted for Heptonstall and Blackshawhead; both these are in West Yorkshire, the pub is only a couple of miles from the county boundary. Wind round with the road, remaining with the main drag and climb the steep, winding hill out of the clough, passing the small huddles of 18th-century – and earlier – cottages. Round the bend at the top of the slope and look for the public footpath sign on the left, pointing along the driveway to Drakeshead Kennels and Cattery.

Follow this driveway for about 100 yards, passing a house and garden on your left, then look carefully for the stone steps set into the high wall on your left. Climb these and then follow the narrow path between spinney and covered reservoir and climb the wall at the end. Just ahead, next to the gate, a further stile marked with two waymark arrows gives access to the field. Once in the field bear half-right, looking to the wall on the near horizon for a narrow gap stile, just to the right of the straggly line of trees. Pass through this gap stile and walk straight ahead. The next stile is in the wall ahead about 10 yards to the right of the dilapidated field gate. Once over this head half-left across the rough pasture heading for the gap in the fence marked by two concrete posts. From here descend the slope heading for the bottom corner of the fir tree plantation on your left; upon reaching this walk downhill for a few yards to leave the field via a small wooden gate in the corner and turn left along the drive.

Within 50 yards look for the stile to the right, immediately before the small bungalow's garden and by the lone telegraph pole. Cross this stile, the footbridge beyond and then the waymarked stile, then walk down the steep slope beyond, keeping to the left of the trees where possible to reach a stream at the bottom. Cross the wooden footbridge beyond yet another stile and turn left, following the path gently up the valley side to join a wider track, going ahead along this. Cross a further stile then another stream and bear left, walking along to reach the hamlet of Hurstwood.

This tiny hamlet retains its old manor house, Hurstwood Hall (built by Barnard Towneley in 1576 for his new bride, Agnes Ormerod, who was all of 10 years old) and the adjoining Manor Farm together with a huddle of mullion windowed ivy-covered cottages and houses. One of these, Spenser's House, is reputed to have been home for a while to the Elizabethan poet Edmund Spenser, contemporary of Shakespeare and author of classic poems such as *The Faerie Queene* and *The Shepheardes Calender*. Another famous resident, this time at the farm, was Richard Tattersall, founder of the horse sales that bear his name. What you miss here on this outward leg you can see on the return journey.

Turn right at the telephone box and walk along the rough road, the Baptist chapel standing proud to your left followed by a terrace of gritstone houses and an old farm. Just past the farm cross the stile and walk up the wide, green, walled path. At the end of the wall bear left and follow the obvious path up out of the valley, largely filled by the fir tree plantation that is now Hurstwood. Go through the metal kissing gate at the top and join the steep path that skirts the edge of the wood. Simply remain with this path, climbing steps and crossing stiles as necessary; glimpses of Hurstwood Reservoir may be had down through the trees on your right.

Cross the stile at the end of the first tract of woodland. Where the waymarkers indicate a split in the path, turn left, following initially a wall on your left and then an obvious path across the moorland pasture. Follow this path across several fields, crossing stiles as appropriate and aim for the right-hand corner of the long, low garage that is the nearest building to you. To the left are extensive views over Burnley to Pendle Hill, further to the right Kelbrook Moor and, in the distance, the southernmost hills of the Yorkshire Dales above Skipton.

Cross the moorland track immediately above the garage and follow the cindered track that leads away beyond it, gaining access to this via two stiles. Stick with this track for the next half mile or so. The hilltop to your right, Wasnop Edge, has an ancient tumulus and a cairn circle on its crest; to your left beyond the small dump, marked by telegraph poles, is the site of a stone circle but there's hardly anything left to see. You'll get to a field gate, to the left of which is a kissing gate made from an old door; go through the kissing gate and walk on with the fence on your right. Eventually the field boundaries funnel in from either side; cross the stile at the far left-hand corner of this funnel and then walk around to the left with the path, keeping the wall to your left. The two reservoirs below are the Swinden Reservoirs, ahead the tiny settlement of Briercliffe. Gradually work down to the field track and follow this to its end, joining the minor road and walking downhill to the bridge.

Turn left immediately before this bridge, pass through the kissing gate and walk along the track alongside the reservoir wall. Up to your right, the multi-windowed building on the crest of the hill is the Roggerham Gate Inn; virtually straight ahead on the hillside the sombre gritstone edifice is Extwistle Hall. This medieval building was left virtually as a shell by a gunpowder explosion in 1717; for

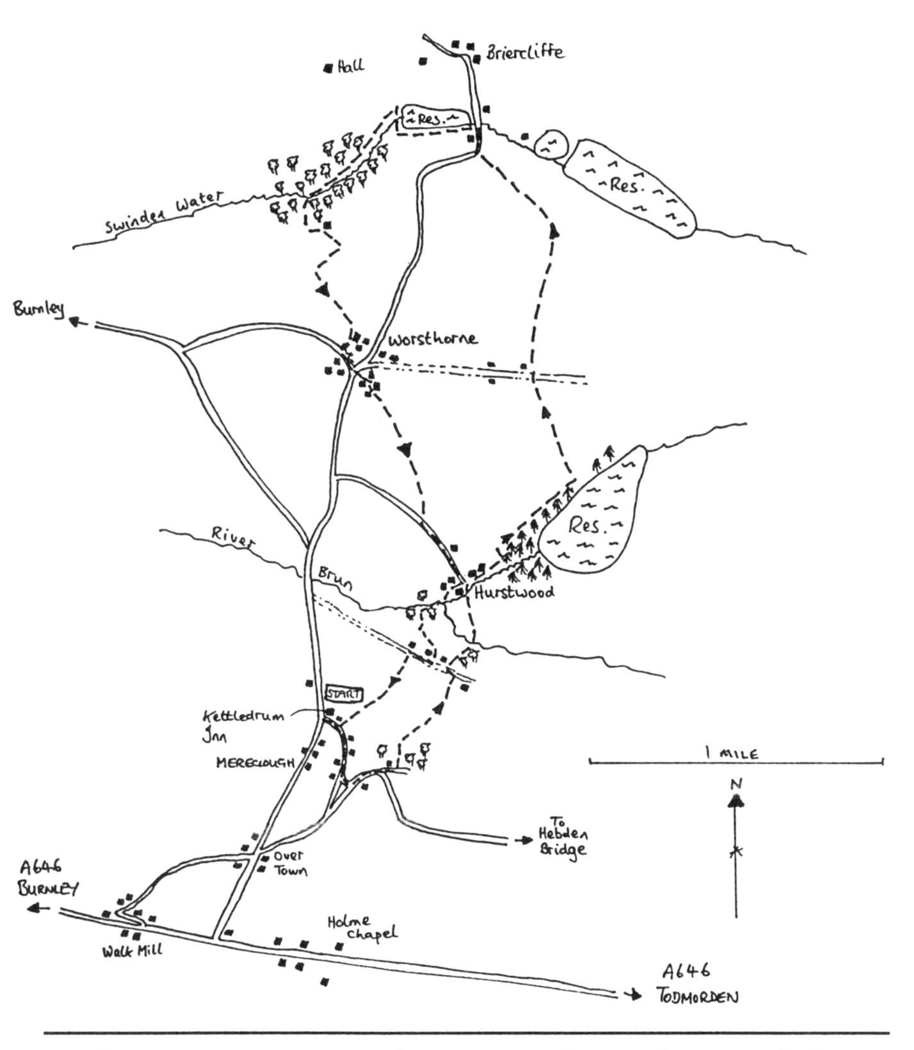

nearly 300 years it was used intermittently as a barn, cattle house and stock feed store before being restored to residential use.

Follow the path across the dam, climb the tall stone step stile at the end and turn left, following the path to, alongside and eventually into the broadleaf woodlands, always remaining to the right of the stream. The clough becomes fairly steep-sided, the path in parts flagged with gritstone blocs. On reaching the wooden post marked with red arrows, go to the left, work down to the stream and cross it on the stepping stones, climbing the steps up the steep valleyside opposite to the pasture at the top. Walk straight ahead to another guidepost, this one with yellow arrows, and turn left, cross the stile and walk on to the drive in front of Wood Hey Farm. Walk along this drive around the double bend and to its end at the playing fields at Worsthorne. At the changing room block turn right and walk along the rough road in front of the terrace. This is Lennox Street; walk along to its end and bear left (not down Gordon Street), remaining with this main village street to reach the village green.

The village of Worsthorne has been much extended but the green remains intact, bordered by church, inn, school and old cottages. You should head half-left to walk between the church on your left and the Bay Horse to your right, then turn right along Green Terrace. Walk to the end then bear left at the two garages and walk along the paved path, a brook to your left, a walled garden on your right. Wind along to the end, go through the kissing gate and into the field. The paved path continues, intermittently, across the field, simply follow it across several fields to emerge on a minor road and turn left along this back down into Hurstwood.

At the centre of the hamlet, turn right in front of the hall and walk towards the farmyard, but turn left before you reach the first cottage and descend the path into the wooded clough. In this wooded clough, it is believed that the 10thcentury Battle of Brunanburgh was fought. Cross the substantial stone footbridge over the River Brun and follow the track, then path, left as it winds up the other side. This becomes a walled footpath, emerging eventually into the edge of a farmyard and in front of the white-painted Rose Cottage. Walk to the left of the hedge, up past the cottage to the farm drive. To the left, at the isolated bungalow, is a small wildlife sanctuary; you should turn right, walk through the area of farmyard buildings and along the drive beyond.

Pass a large house on your right and you will soon reach a hangar of beech trees, also on the right. On your left here is a stone stile into a field. Go over this and follow the well-used path down the dry valley, crossing a further stile on your right a short while later. Continue along the path towards the buildings ahead, bearing slightly right as you approach them to take the stile leading into the grounds of Mereclough Barn (*not* Mereclough House). Upon reaching the road beyond, turn right uphill to return to The Kettledrum Inn.

22. North Lune: Hornby

Route: Hornby – Loyn Bridge – Arkholme – Gressingham – The Snab

Distance: 8 miles

Maps: Explorer sheets OL7 (English Lakes, SE) & OL41 (Forest of Bowland)

Start: The Royal Oak, Main Street, Hornby LA2 8JU

Access: Hornby is on the A683 Lancaster to Kirkby Lonsdale road about nine miles north east of Lancaster, seven miles north east of Junction 34 on the M6 (Lancaster North and Morecambe turn). The Royal Oak is on the left at the northern end of the village.

The Royal Oak (015242 21228)

This old, stone-built roadside inn is a listed building and dates from 1781, a stone plaque built into the front of the building records that it was built in that year for William and Emma Gelderd. Presumably they were also farmers as the pub was only half of the size it is today; a barn survived in use until after the second war when it was put to use as a café, eventually being incorporated into the pub proper in the late 1960s when local Lancaster brewers Yates and Jackson took over from Bass. They largely gutted the old pub and generated their ideal of a comfortable village local, the results of which remain largely unchanged today. The brewery sold up in 1984; Thwaites of Blackburn took over many of their pubs including this one, where landlord Philip Gaskell keeps an exceptional pint of their award winning bitter.

The one-roomed pub features a lot of exposed stonework, liberally dressed with brasses, plates, Toby jugs and the occasional oddment or two. The games area is largely separate from the main area that is laid out with "traditional" pub moquette chairs and low tables together with a few wall seats and high-backed benches to one end. The Royal Oak is open from 11.30am – 11.00pm, Mon-Sat and noon – 10.30pm on Sunday. Bar meals are served all day and children are very welcome. The main theme of the pub is maritime/navy, the name 'Royal Oak' coming from the battleship that was scuppered in Scapa Flow, Orkneys during the Second World War.

Hornby

Dominating the village is the extravagant castle, Victorian exuberance at its best (or worst), embattlements and turrets leap-frogging each other ever higher above the wooded slopes of the River Wenning; perhaps Disney once paid a call. The original 13th-century pele tower is buried somewhere within the pile which originally was the home of the Stanley family. Sir Edward Stanley commanded a contingent of troops at the battle of Flodden Field (in Northumberland) in 1513, this victory over the Scots earned him the title Lord Monteagle. The Stanleys are long gone; the castle has passed through the hands of a string of owners and is now a private residence not open to the public. It is best viewed either from the village's bridge or from the main road to the south-west, with a low evening sun highlighting the grey/red sandstone in which it is built.

Hornby Castle

The village itself is little more than a long main street leading to a bridge over the Wenning, the houses and cottages are largely Georgian in origin. The church of St Margaret's acted as the castle's chapel; it has a very rare octagonal tower built for Sir Edward as thanks for his deliverance from, and victory at, Flodden. The large drinking fountain at the road junction south of the river is dated 1858; the playful badge attached recalls a former owner of the castle, Pudsey Dawson, who introduced myriad cats into the castle, then uninhabited, to rid it of a plague of rats. Priory Farm, standing alone on its knoll above the Lune just west of the village, is the site of a medieval priory, the only remnant of which is part of a Saxon cross now housed in St Margaret's church.

Nearby, Gressingham huddles in the narrow neck of Gressingham Beck. Many of the cottages date from Stuart times although the village is recorded in Domesday. The church originates from Saxon times and houses a cross dating from 850; the adjoining hall dates from 1688, a squat three-storey building with fine mullioned windows. The beck winds down the centre of the hamlet in a deep, winding cleft.

North Lune

Using a geological generalisation the River Lune divides an outlying bloc of mountain limestone (more familiar as the dominant rock of the Yorkshire Dales) from the gritstone massif of Bowland. North-west of the river this area of Lancashire is characterised by typical limestone scenery, a craggy landscape bounded by extensive limestone "pavements" and with few surface streams. This geology results in a distinct flora, ash woodlands predominate and the vivid green grass is rich with lime loving plants: lily-of-the-valley, hawkbit and knapweed for example. The buildings, too, have that characteristic, mellow, light colouring in contrast to the dour gritstone of much of the county; compare the villages north of Morecambe with those east of Preston, for example. The Lune itself is one of the cleanest rivers in Britain and has one of the best salmon runs; a week's fishing can well run into four figures. The artist J.M.W. Turner was captivated by the river, one of his most famous landscapes was painted at the Crook of Lune, just east of Lancaster. To the west of this city the river sweeps into Morecambe Bay through some of the most extensive sandbanks and salt marshes in the country; to the north most of the coastline is either nature reserve or AONB.

The Walk

Walk up Hornby's one main street and at the junction at the top bear left towards Gressingham. Wind along and down this minor road for about half a mile to reach the narrow old Loyn Bridge across the Lune. Just before you bend round to this, a stile on your right leads to a path up to an old pill box in the field, behind which is the excellently preserved motte and bailey castle, Castle Stede. The motte, or mound, at the far end is now capped with trees and the bailey, or enclosure, is very well defined; you are on a public footpath so linger to appreciate the site.

Return to Loyn Bridge and cross it, walk along past the lay-by and enter the field on the right at the signpost to Thrushgill Wood and Arkholme. For the next two miles, follow the Lune upstream, passing through Thrushgill Wood and several other copses and leaving the riverbank from time to time as the obvious line of path dictates your course. Views ahead and to the right are spectacular and remain with you throughout the walk. You get an unusual angle on Ingleborough, its sculptured northern face dominating the Pennine edge far behind the village of Melling. Peeking out behind and beyond this, the sharp edge of Pen-y-Ghent cuts the distant horizon whilst to the north the gentler rounded tops of Leck Fell (at just over 2000ft the highest point in Lancashire) and the southern end of the Howgill Fells dominate the horizon.

You can see the village of Arkholme ahead of you on a low ridge above the river. Aim to pass to the right of the white house that stands at the foot of this ridge near the riverbank. Beyond this are two cottages; at the foot of their garden a stile leads past a field gate onto a track that curves up to the left and becomes the one village street of Arkholme. First right off this street will take you to the tiny St John's Chapel and beyond this the motte of an old castle; the views from the footpath here are excellent. Return to the village street and walk up it. The street is lined with myriad old cottages, barns and farmhouses, many with dates on their lintel or corbel stone going back to the early 1600s. At the top of the street turn left along the main road (the Bay Horse pub, opposite, is a useful half-way stop and has several real ales).

Walk along the footpath to the second public footpath sign on the right. Turn right into the drive leading up to the farmyard, pass

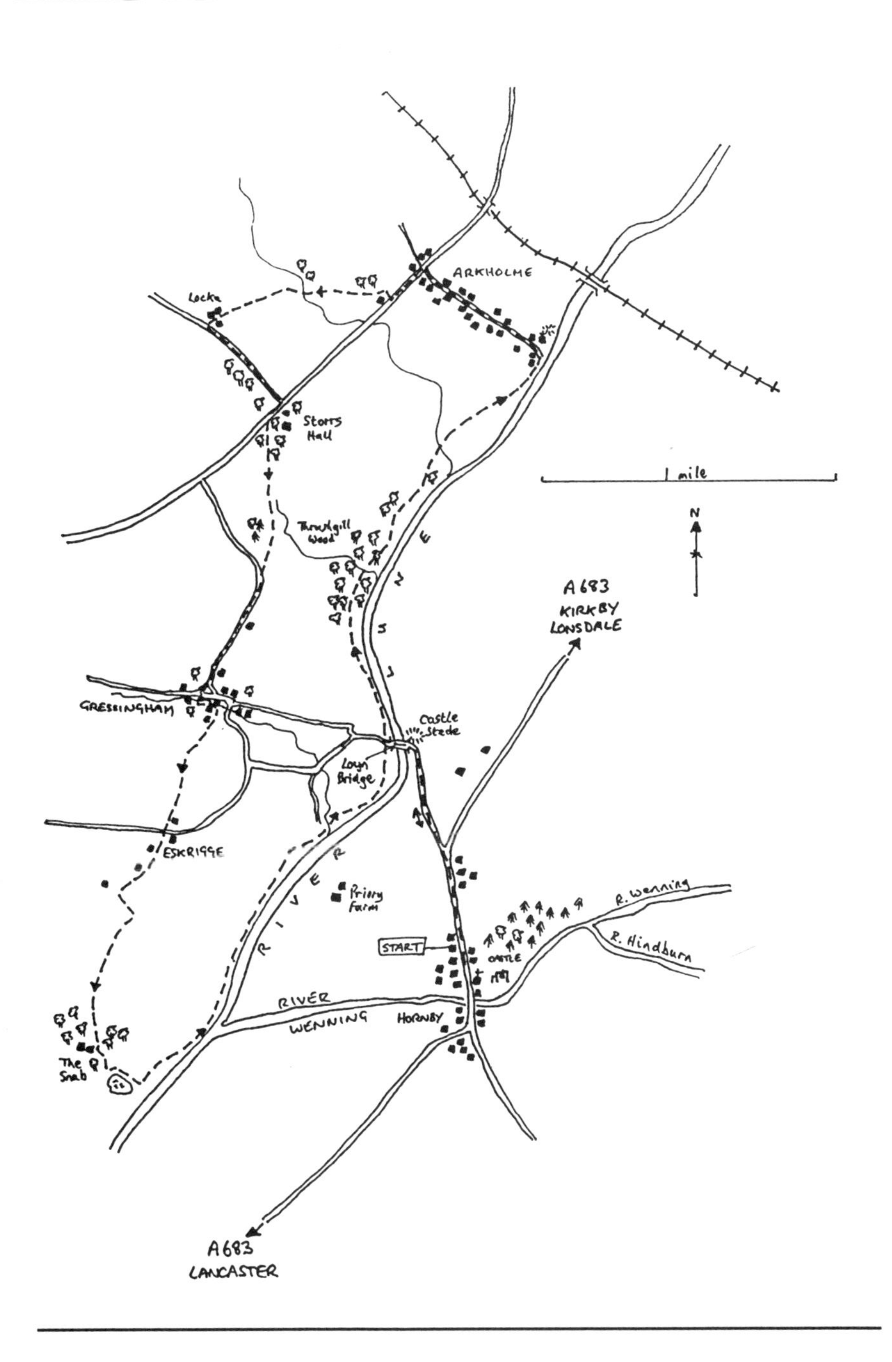
ARKHOLME
Locka
Storrs Hall
1 mile
N
Throdgill Wood
A 683
KIRKBY
LONSDALE
GRESSINGHAM
Castle Stede
Loyn Bridge
ESKRIGGE
Priory Farm
R. Wenning
R. Hindburn
START
CASTLE
RIVER
WENNING
HORNBY
The Snab
A 683
LANCASTER

through the first gate about 30 yards along and look for the stile on your right. Cross this and skirt the farmyard, passing through the gap stile beside the gate at the far end. From here, walk across the field, heading for the left-hand side of the line of trees at the far side. Go through the gate next to these trees and follow the track up the left-hand side of the next field. Look for the footbridge on your left a couple of yards to the left of the wooden post that stands isolated towards the edge of the field. From the stile at the far end of the footbridge take a bearing on the roof of the house that pokes out above the near-hillside and walk up towards this. Go through the gate in the wire fence and then enter the small paddock beside the house. Leave this by the gate at the far side and walk up around the house, across the gritted yard in front of the cottages and to the minor road. Turn left along this and walk down to the main road.

On reaching the main road turn right and cross it. In the estate to the left is the gothic-style mansion of Storrs Hall; the cottage at the gatehouse has a date stone of 1743. Pass the entrance drive to the hall and then go left through the green door in the wall at the public footpath sign. Walk along the short, railed section and climb the stile at the end. From here look half-right to locate a stile in the wire fence, walk to and climb this and then aim for a second stile on the hill top about 50 yards to the left of the birch and fir plantation. Once over this veer slightly right to reach the field gate in the corner beside a small copse. Go over the stile beside this and walk left down the narrow road to the hamlet of Gressingham.

At the fork bear right and walk over the shoulder of the hill down to the T-junction. Cross virtually straight over here, going down the lane beside the telephone box to the series of railed paths and footbridges across the stream. Walk across these and up the path at the far side, turning left along the narrow road at the top. In less than 100 yards look on the right for a yellow waymark arrow pointing up a drive guarded by an unusual wooden gate. Go up here, through the gate at the end and up the narrow paddock beyond, at the end of which is a stile in the left-hand corner. Cross this and head for the oak tree in the top right corner of the field. Climb the stile beneath this and walk steeply uphill to the top right corner of this field, near which a further stile leads into a long paddock. At the far end of this cross through the wire fence (using the wire mesh gate) and walk to the field gate beyond. Once through this walk along the farm track to the minor road.

This is the scattered community of Eskrigge. Go straight across the road and along the track opposite. Walk in front of the rebuilt cottages and through the gate beyond, sticking to the right-hand boundary and passing the barn conversion. At the end of the field climb the fence stile and bear right to the stone gateposts. Go left up the old lane here and in a matter of yards fork left beneath the holly trees. Walk up this sunken lane to the top and bear right along the line of fence, keeping it on your left for about 100 yards. At the rusty field gate that you meet head-on at the offset field corner enter the field the gate leads into, follow the hedge to the hilltop and then down the other side. Down to your left is the gravelly confluence of the Wenning with the Lune.

On reaching the field corner by the large oak tree pass through the gate and bear half-left down the field towards the fence to the left of the barn. Cross the stile and pass to the left of the barn. Go through the gate at the end and turn left, following the rough, then surfaced drive leading away from the house called The Snab. After about 100 yards go through the gate on your left, marked with a waymark arrow. Walk down the slope and then turn right, passing the large pond to your right that is well populated with swans, Canada and pink-footed geese and duck. You are heading for the riverbank about 50 yards to the right of the isolated hut. Cross the stile here and then walk upstream. From here, simply follow the riverside path, diverging with it as necessary to reach Loyn Bridge some distance upstream, crossing the bridge to return to Hornby.

23. North Lune: Overton

Route: Overton – Bazil Point – Sunderland Point – Potts Corner

Distance: 6.5 miles

Map: Explorer 296, Lancaster, Morecambe & Fleetwood

Start: The Ship Hotel, Overton, near Lancaster LA3 3HD

Access: From Lancaster take the A589 towards Morecambe and turn off at the new roundabout along the B5273 towards Heysham. At the mini-roundabout take the exit signposted to Middleton and Overton (N.B. this is a tide-affected road). Pass the Golden Ball pub and continue along this road, turning left just before the line of pylons crosses the road to reach Overton. The pub is beside the village's main street. If the road is flooded by the tide then return to the B5273 and drive through to Heysham, following the signs for the docks. Just before the docks, where the main road bends sharp right at traffic lights, continue straight ahead to Middleton and thence Overton.

The Ship Hotel (01524 858231)

The Ship is rather akin to Dr Who's Tardis: a time capsule containing a lot more than would seem possible at a cursory glance from outside. Apart from the cigarette and fruit machines (and the modest price of the beer) time stopped late last century. A glorious Victorian polished wood bar, complete with glass architraves, remains the focal point, bedecked with a range of handpumps offering Daniel Thwaites Bitter. To discover the pub's hidden depths, however, climb the steps beside the bar and venture a look at an incredible collection of birds' eggs and stuffed birds. These pastimes were common amongst the Victorian gentry and the collection amassed at The Ship must be typical of such; I doubt, however, whether the display in the snug can have a rival anywhere.

The rest of the furnishings reflect the Victorian era, comfortable settees, old solid chairs and tables, long-case clocks and a muted collection of brasses and pictures. The current licensees, Mr & Mrs Webber, have been at The Ship for only a few short years. They have a hard act to follow in the shape of Ma McKlusky. This formidable lady was the licensee for over 50 years early last century. Her word was law; her reputation at dealing with drunks – ejecting brawling sailors two at a time for example – legendary. The pub was known locally as Ma McKlusky's, her Edwardian principles well respected by (almost) all who used the pub. The Webbers extend a warm and friendly welcome to all-comers, and home-made food and bar snacks are always available. The pub is open from 11.30am to 11pm Mon-Sat, and from 12 noon to 10.30pm on Sunday.

Sunderland Point

The River Lune empties into Morecambe Bay a few miles south west of Lancaster. Along the western side of the estuary a narrow spit of land has, over the centuries, survived the combined erosive efforts of the river and the sea. Rising a matter of but a few feet above the surrounding salt marshes, this is the Sunderland promontory.

Like its more famous namesake in the north east, Sunderland was once an important port. Unlike its namesake, however, the lifeblood of Lancashire's Sunderland was not shipbuilding but more general cargoes and with more than a passing interest in the slave trade. Whether slaves were ever actually incarcerated in the small warehouses, some of which survive as private dwellings, as some commentators have suggested is a moot point. Certainly Sunderland benefited indirectly from slavery; it is claimed that the first bales of American cotton to reach these Islands were shipped through the port. An old house on the promontory is named Cotton Tree House, the large tree growing by its front door is said to be a cotton tree, germinated from a seed which fell from one of these bales (I've also seen it described as a black oak, a black poplar and a kapok). Other cargoes included hardwood, molasses, tobacco and gunpowder.

Established by the Quaker merchant Robert Lawson, Sunderland acted as the port for Lancaster and was busy as such by the early 1700s; seagoing vessels preferred the moorings of Sunderland to the tortuous and treacherous approach up the Lune to Lancaster. Cargoes were offloaded and stored at Sunderland before continuing overland or by lighter to the old county town. Fortunes were made by merchants based at Sunderland at the expense of those trading from Lancaster; this led to the development of the rival Glasson Dock in the early 1800s which in turn resulted in the very rapid decline of Sunderland, virtually all its trade was lost and only a few fishing smacks remained.

Today it is difficult to imagine Sunderland as a busy port. The moorings have gone, the channel is largely silted up; warehouses, stores and the tavern are now private houses or have disappeared completely. What remains is a strand of cottages and houses along a sandy road on the leeward side of the promontory cut off at high tide from the rest of Lancashire when the narrow road through the marshes is underwater. Even the post box is emptied only when tidal conditions allow. A few yachts and fishing cobles still use the foreshore as a base but essentially the hamlet is now a quiet backwater on the lonely, windswept promontory, a seventh heaven for birdwatchers and those seeking a day completely away from it all.

The Walk

Walk uphill from the pub for a few yards and turn left along Chapel View. Pass by the renovated barn on your right and turn right up the footpath signposted for Hall Greaves and Chapel Lane, then keeping left at each opportunity to emerge eventually on a surfaced road. Turn right down this and, at the junction by the post box, go straight ahead. Keep left at the fork, pass the houses to your right and walk along the track across the field, crossing a cattle grid to reach the front of a pebble-dashed cottage.

At this point, look to your left to find the public footpath that descends the steps and goes along the foreshore, soon passing below a further cottage. From here, there are excellent views across the estuary to Glasson Dock. Simply follow the shoreline around to reach Bazil Point; you can see the shipping channel marked out from Glasson whilst the houses across the water ahead are at Sunderland. Remain on the foreshore and turn your back on the estuary, walking now along the edge of the salt marsh to your left; there are public footpaths both on the land side and marsh side of the fence, the choice is yours as they both end up at the same spot, a white ladder stile leading onto a path which goes up over the hill and back to Overton. You, however, should not climb this stile but instead remain beside the marsh, picking your way along to the surfaced road a few hundred yards further on. On reaching this road, you have a choice. If the tide is on its way out or is at low water then you can simply turn left here and walk along the road across the marshes to

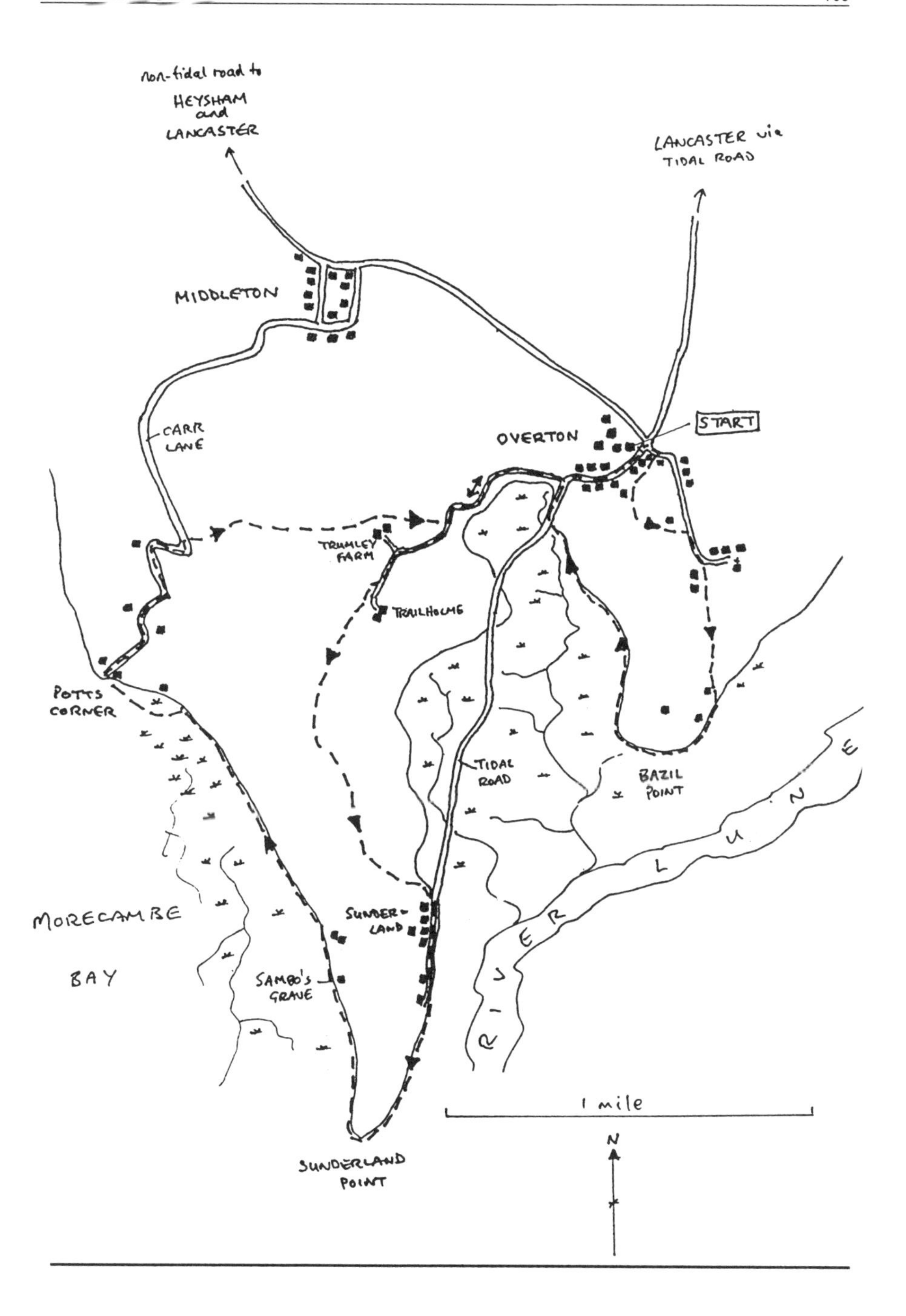
non-tidal road to
HEYSHAM
and
LANCASTER
LANCASTER via
TIDAL ROAD
MIDDLETON
START
OVERTON
CARR
LANE
TRUMLEY
FARM
TRAILHOLME
POTTS
CORNER
TIDAL
ROAD
BAZIL
POINT
RIVER LUNE
MORECAMBE
BAY
SUNDER-
LAND
SAMBO'S
GRAVE
SUNDERLAND
POINT
1 mile
N

Sunderland. If, however, the tide is on its way in or fully up then this road will be flooded. In this case turn right and walk up over the bank to the junction.

Turn left at this junction along the road signposted "cul de sac" and follow it, bearing left at every opportunity. You'll end up walking along a concrete-surfaced farm drive towards Trailholme – look for the small white guidepost. Walk along this drive, ignoring the public footpath sign on your right after just a few paces. About 20 yards before the track swings left to approach the farm is a stile through the hedge on your right. Go over this, turn left and follow the field boundary along two fields. At the end of the second field go through the gate and turn right, walking along the slab-surfaced path alongside the barbed wire fence. At the end cross the small stile on your left and walk along the bank to the white ladder stile. Once over this look to the diagonally opposite corner of the field (virtually straight ahead of you), walk to and climb the further white ladder stile there. From here, walk half-left across the field to the footbridge in the far-left corner. Cross it (mind the cross-bolts, presumably there to stop agile animals from crossing) and then remain with the field drain, crossing a further two bridges. The subsequent bridge you will reach is derelict, the ditch having been filled in. From this spot head half-left to the fence across the levee (bank), then climb the sets of steps to access the foreshore and walk along to Sunderland.

Remain with the road (which is a public footpath) and walk past the strand of cottages and houses, passing the cotton tree and, eventually, the Old Hall. Beyond the Old Hall walk along the concreted edge of the green to gain access to the foreshore (the area between high tide mark and low tide mark is public domain) and walk along the pebbly beach to the end of the promontory at Sunderland Point.

The prospect from the point is both diverse and extensive. Straight ahead is the Wyre, the tall chimney marks the ICI works at Fleetwood. Nearer to hand, the lighthouse is Plover Scar Light, marking the shipping channel up to Glasson and Lancaster; the squat, slightly askew building on the shore near this is the chapter house of Cockersand Abbey. To your left, the line of the Forest of Bowland dominates the horizon; the white buildings on the hillside nearer to hand are Lancaster University. To the north of these, you can pick out the domed Ashton Memorial in Lancaster. Close at hand, the estuary teems with wildfowl of every shape, size and colour; tiny knot to large heron, colourful and noisy oystercatcher and shellduck, silent and deadly little owl and hawks.

Continue round the point and walk northwards along the shoreline. Ahead is the reactor of Heysham Power Station, beyond which the mountains of southern Lakeland form a spectacular skyline. The ferries you may see operate year-round to the Isle of Man whilst far out to sea the keen-eyed should pick out some of the gas rigs on the Morecambe Bay natural gas field. Several minutes walk will bring you to the enclosure, on your right, of Sambo's Grave, a small white cross and a poignant epitaph stamped on a brass plaque marking the site of the grave of this unfortunate African servant. He died here at the brewhouse in Sunderland after his master left him here whilst he himself went away on business. Sambo didn't understand English, refused all food and died of a broken heart, seemingly abandoned by his master. Alternatively, he was taken gravely ill aboard ship whilst anchored at the point and died before any medical help could be administered. Either way he was buried in unconsecrated ground some distance from the small chapel at Sunderland.

From the grave, continue along the foreshore, for the next mile or so bordering the extensive salt marshes to end up at Potts Corner, the second cottage you come to. You can reach this either by following the path along the shoreline or along the track you come to which winds out across the marshes to end up near the cottage.

Immediately beyond the cottage turn right and walk along the lane, Carr Lane, passing a number of bungalows and the entrance to a caravan park. Stick with the lane as it winds round several bends until you reach a very sharp left-hand bend. Just round this on the right is a public footpath sign to Middleton. Take this and walk along to the white stile, climb this and then follow the edge of the field on your right. Climb a further stile and then head across the pastures towards Trumley Farm. You'll see a stile through the fence about 20 yards to the left of the farm, cross this and aim for the next stile which is beside the area of infill tipping; work across this to a further stile, from which walk across the field to the ladder stile at the far side. This gives access to the marshland road followed earlier in the walk – simply turn left and walk along it back to Overton. Pass the Globe Inn on your right and bear right up the road to return to The Ship Hotel.

24. North Lune: Warton

Route: Warton – Warton Crag – Crag Foot – Jenny Brown's Point – Silverdale Green – Leighton Moss

Distance: 7 miles

Map: Explorer OL7, The English Lakes (South eastern area)

Start: The George Washington, Warton, Carnforth LA5 9PJ

Access: Warton is about seven miles north of Lancaster, just west of the A6 and M6 roads. Leave the M6 at Junction 35 and go along the motorway spur to the roundabout on the A6. Turn right here, following the Milnthorpe sign. In about 200 yards (and before you reach the next roundabout) a narrow road on your left is signposted for Warton. Drive along this, Borwick Lane, and turn left at the end, along the village's main street, to reach the Black Bull a further quarter of a mile away. There is ample parking at the pub or at a car park up the narrow road beside the pub.

By rail, you can pick up this walk at Silverdale station; this is on the Preston/Lancaster to Barrow in Furness line and has an infrequent daily service.

The George Washington (01524 732865)

No one seems quite sure how old the building is or how long it has served as a pub; the consensus is that the 15th century is a reliable guess for both. The white painted, three-storey building is certainly a respectable age, bedecked with chimneys and dominating the tiny village square just a stone's throw away from the church. One end of the main bar room is dominated by a huge brick fireplace; the fire helps light the area which is served only by a series of small, wood panelled windows, causing heavy shadows on the low, heavily beamed ceiling at this end of the pub. Or take your refreshment outside into the beer garden.

A large collection of old plates and carving dishes adorns shelves around the walls whilst the bar sports a range of cask beers including Boddingtons and Worthington's bitters. The George Washington has a reputation locally for the home-cooked meals that form a very extensive menu for both restaurant and bar meals. Food is served each lunchtime except Mondays (Tue-Thu, noon – 2.30pm and 5.00 – 7.30pm, Fri-Sun, noon – 7.30pm).

Opening hours are Mon, 3.00pm – 11.00pm; Tue-Sat, noon – 11.00pm and Sun, noon – 10.30pm. Accommodation is provided in six guest rooms – three being en-suite.

Warton

The village is dominated by Warton Crag, one of the great reefs of limestone that tower above the coast at the northern end of Morecambe Bay and around the Kent estuary. Viewed from a distance the southern face of the crag is a series of giant steps leading down to the salt marshes; the lower one has been heavily quarried but the upper ones are natural scars, reflecting the way the limestone was laid down in a warm sea 300 million years ago. The Crag, together with the marshes and much of the limestone coast to the north-west, form the Arnside & Silverdale Area of Outstanding Natural Beauty.

Warton has seen a lot of development in the past few decades and now acts largely as a commuter town for Carnforth, Lancaster and Preston. The long, winding main street and a few adjoining folds remain as a reminder of the long history of the village. Main Street is liberally dotted with old yeoman's cottages and rows of tiny pebbledashed cottages whose windows alone give away their antiquity. Near the post office is Washington House, once home to the family that produced the first President of the newly independent American Colonies. Another politician with links to the village, by marriage, was Winston Churchill. Detailed family trees of both gentlemen are displayed in St Oswald's church whose solid tower was built by a member of the Washington family in the 15th century; much of the church is somewhat younger than this. Downhill from the church are the remains of a 14th-century rectory, now in the care of English Heritage and open daily except Mondays.

The Walk

If you've got, or can beg or borrow, a pair of binoculars then ensure that you take them on this walk – it is probably the best one for wild birds and views in this book.

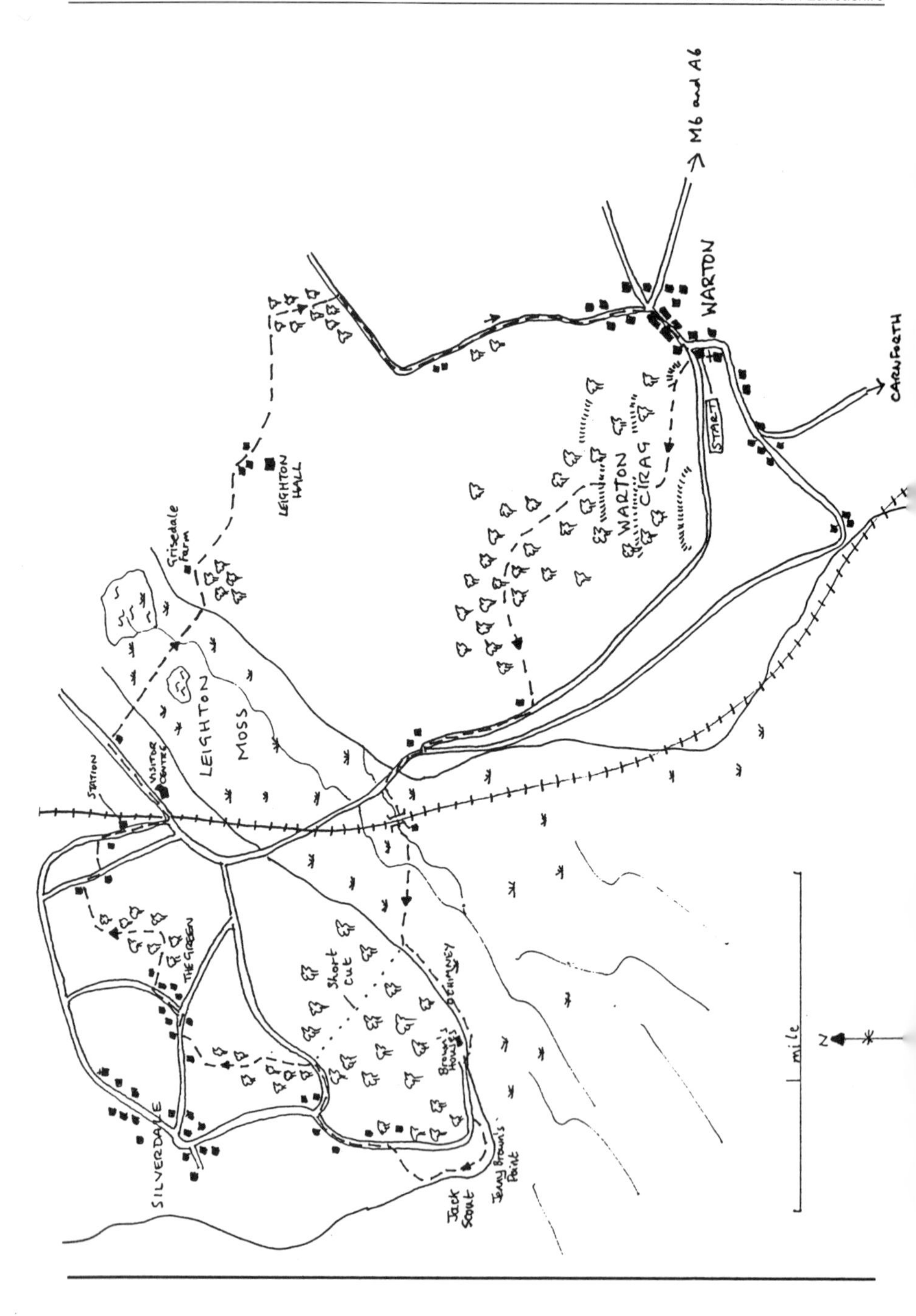
M6 and A6
WARTON
CARNFORTH
START
WARTON CRAG
LEIGHTON HALL
Grisedale Farm
LEIGHTON MOSS
STATION
VISITOR CENTRE
THE GREEN
Short cut
CHIMNEY
Brown's Houses
SILVERDALE
Jack Scout
Jenny Brown's Point
mile
N

Walk up the narrow lane beside the pub, Crag Road, and angle right into the small car park a short distance up on the right. From the back of this car park walk up the rough path through the scrubby woodland to the gap stile at the top beside the information board (which outlines the attractions of the crag area). Turn right and then left a few paces later to follow the path that takes you gradually uphill. You're walking along one of the steps along the south face of the Crag, the immense views take in the coastline for many miles to the south, the fells of the Forest of Bowland and, as you climb higher, the southern edges of the Lake District.

Cross the stile at the top and walk ahead with the fence on your left. Look to your right for some large boulders of limestone perched on a small rise. You need to pass a few yards to the right of these and walk across the depression ahead to a large wooden stile. Beyond this scramble up the path to the next small plateau and continue to head for the highest point of the crag. Walking to this may prove a little tricky as the area is well-blessed with thorn trees and scrubby ash and the ground surface is a jigsaw of limestone blocks and hollows. These are a common feature of limestone areas and reflect differential weathering of the rock, the small ridges are called clints and the fissures between known as grikes. At the right time of year these grikes will be rich with lime loving plants and flowers; Warton Crag is well known for its wildflowers and for the butterflies and moths which make use of such.

At the summit of the crag, you will find a triangulation pillar and a wooden beacon pole. The pillar is one of thousands throughout the country upon which the Ordnance Survey base their maps, "triangulating" with neighbouring pillars to build up an accurate picture of the shape of the countryside and towns. The pillar upon which all the other ones are homed is on a down above Portsmouth whilst all heights are based on mean (average) sea level at Newlyn Harbour in Cornwall. The summit of the crag has been recognised as the site of an old British hillfort although remains are, frankly, scant.

The path you should leave the summit by goes north from a point between the pillar and the beacon pole. It's an obvious path and within 50 yards you will come to a signpost offering a choice of route to either Coach Road, Warton or Crag Foot. Follow the Crag Foot sign and walk off gently down through the trees, largely ash with a generous sprinkling of yew and holly. Remain with the path as it winds slowly down from the summit, following the occasional directional sign for Crag Foot. In a few hundred yards you will reach a rough, walled road known as Occupation Road. Turn left along this and walk to the end about half a mile distant, enjoying the ever-increasing views across the Kent Estuary.

On reaching the end turn right and walk along down the minor road to the junction at the bottom. Go straight ahead here and then bear left and follow the main road out across the mosslands. The vast, flat area to your right is Leighton Moss, one of England's premiere nature reserves, of which more later. On reaching the sharp right-hand bend turn left along the track and walk along beside the drainage ditch. Pass under the railway bridge – carrying the spectacular Cumbrian coastline that still has regular steam-hauled services during the summer – and then turn right across the solid stone bridge, essentially the sluice gate to this particular drain. Cross the gate at the far end and turn left along the embankment. Cross the stile and walk along left to a further stile, cross this and then bear right with the embankment, following it across this huge expanse of mosslands, its line marked by occasional thorn trees. The area is a paradise for birdwatchers with hundreds of oystercatcher, dunlin, greenshank, curlew, shellduck and myriad other wading birds.

At the far end of the embankment is a signpost; you should turn left towards Jenny Brown's Point. If, however, you wish to avoid this mile or so of largely coastal walk then go straight ahead with the sign towards Woodwell and walk over the hilltop to rejoin the walk later.

Having turned left follow the path along the shoreline, cross the stile and continue along towards the point. Stick close to the shore as the area of flats and sands to your left is known, with good reason, as Quicksand Pool. On a clear day the bulk of the Forest of Bowland beyond Warton seems almost close enough to touch. Pass by the forlorn, isolated chimney (evidence, together with one passed on the other side of the moss, of the copper smelting which once took place locally) at the edge of the marshes and walk along the foreshore in front of Brown's Houses, gaining the narrow road just beyond and following this above the shoreline. In a couple of hundred yards go through the kissing gate on your left and walk onto the low headland of Jack Scout, an area of National Trust land (use the donation box at your discretion). This is a limestone knoll that offers increasingly spectacular views up into the mountains around Coniston the fur-

Brown's Houses and old smelting chimney

ther round you walk. Jenny Brown's Point, named after an old woman who lived in the isolated cottages on the foreshore, is the southerly point of this knoll.

Cut back inland, along the line of the wall if not before, and rejoin the minor road, turning left along this to walk past the folly-like Lindeth Tower (home, for a short time, to the celebrated Victorian novelist Mrs Gaskell) to the road junction. Turn right here up along Hollins Lane towards Carnforth. Follow this road along past the craft centre and walk up the short, steep slope into the trees. On your right you'll find a signpost directing you towards Crag Foot – this is where the short cut from the end of the embankment comes out. On your left is a sign for Woodwell; take this path, favouring the upper route, along this limestone ridge. Remain with the path through the woods, initially with a pasture to your right and a steep drop on your left, and bear gradually left with it. You should soon find yourself at a stile into a narrow pasture. Cross into this pasture, bear right and walk to the signpost on the bank top, from there following the direction indicated to The Green, essentially left. Cross the stile at the end and walk on along the edge of the woods with a wall to your right. On reaching the green door in the wall turn right and walk along the walled/fenced path. Cross the stone step stile at the end, walk along the walled track to the minor road at the end and turn right to Silverdale Green.

In about 100 yards, turn left along Bottoms Lane, towards Arnside and Milnthorpe. Just past the last house on the right take the path signposted to Burton Well and walk along the track that soon deteriorates into a walled path. Burton Well itself is in the walled enclosure off to the right at the end of this track and below the limestone cliff. You should cross the stile here and walk along to the footbridge; cross this and walk across Lambert's Meadow to the ladder stile at the woodland edge. Climb the stile and turn left, walking up the steep, stepped path into and through the woods. At the crossing of paths go straight ahead, pass beside the garage and walk to the road at the end, turning right along this.

Within 50 yards, a worn footpath sign points the way, left, across the golf course. There are occasional red and white route markers but, essentially, aim to pass to the left of the two small, bare knolls but to the right of the one capped with fir trees – and beware of projectiles. Climb the stile to the left of the gate at the far side of the course and turn right along the road, soon passing Silverdale Station on your left. A short while later turn left, cross the railway bridge and walk down to the Leighton Moss Visitor Centre.

Leighton Moss

The Visitor Centre and Leighton Moss are owned by the RSPB. The Moss is one of the society's major reserves, its principal attractions are the very rare marsh harrier and bittern, together with an amazing variety of migratory water birds and rare warblers. The vast area of ponds, drains and reedbeds are also home to otters whilst red squirrels and deer live in adjoining woodlands. Until 1917 the mossland was kept drained by a series of ditches and pumps and provided rich farmland, since then it has been allowed to revert to the semi-natural state you see today. The reserve is open from 9.00am – 9.00pm daily (dusk if earlier) and permits are available from the visitor centre shop; there's also a café here (you don't need a permit to use the public footpath that this walk follows across the moss).

Continue along the road away from the visitor centre and start to walk uphill with it. Immediately past the cottage on your right a track falls away down onto the Moss; walk down along this and out across Leighton Moss, this is the only public footpath across it. High reeds and bulrushes, dogwood, goat willow, spindle and alder trees thickly border the track. Here and there gaps have been created offering views across the ponds and meres; about half way across is a public hide which offers uninterrupted views across the largest stretch of water. At the far end go through the gate and follow the field track along to and past Grisedale Farm, then remain with the surfaced road to end up beside Leighton Hall. This spectacular neo-Gothic mansion was created around an old fortified manor house. It was renovated in this style by a member of the Gillow family (of the Waring & Gillow furniture company) and contains fine period furniture. The Hall is open daily (not Sat. or Mon. except Bank Holiday Mondays) from 2pm (12.30pm in August) to 5pm between May and September; an additional attraction is a display of free-flying eagles and falconry, on weather-suitable afternoons, at 3.30pm.

As the sign attached to the barn indicates, the public footpath cuts up the hillside to the left of the driveway leading to the hall. Follow the line of telegraph poles up the hillside, passing to the left of the enclosure of trees half way up the slope. At the top turn right and walk along the line of trees that feather the spine of this ridgetop. The bare bones of this spine are exposed boulders and lumps of the underlying limestone. At the end climb the stile behind the green wooden fencing and follow the path through the woods to the minor road. Turn right down this and follow it all the way back to Warton village, about a mile away. Turn right at the main road to return to The George Washington.

The River Darwen, in the Darwen Gorge
– on the Riley Green walk (see pages 38 to 43)

Also of Interest:

BEST PUB WALKS IN THE LAKE DISTRICT

Neil Coates

This, the longest-established (and best-researched) pub walks book for the Lakes, is amazingly wide-ranging, with an emphasis on quality of walks and the real ale rewards that follow! *£6.95*

BEST PUB WALKS in the LAKELAND FRINGES

Neil Coates

"This is the best way to enjoy a country walk, and advice on such not too tough walks and pubs in areas around the edge of the Lake District are provided in this excellent new paperback." NW EVENING MAIL *£6.95*

DISCOVERY WALKS IN LANCASHIRE

Brian Conduit

Walks with a heritage theme: Roman remains, medieval castles and abbeys, nature reserves, country parks and the many monuments to the county's role in the industrial revolution. "An impressive variety of walks ... rounded off with some fascinating details on interesting features" BLACKPOOL GAZETTE. *£6.95*

LANCASHIRE MAGIC & MYSTERY

Kenneth Fields

Covering all of Lancashire, including Merseyside and Greater Manchester, here are tales of hauntings, witchcraft, religious relics, folklore and UFOs – a must for anyone interested in the supernatural. *£6.95*

WEST PENNINE WALKS

Mike Cresswell;
photographs Reg Timms

Bolton's Mike Cresswell is renowned for the accuracy of his instructions and his impish humour. Here, he explores the countryside of the delightful West Pennine area. *£7.95*

WALKS IN MYSTERIOUS LANCASHIRE

Graham Dugdale

30 walks, all excellent in their own right, inextricably linked with Lancashire history and legends. Lucid walking directions and the author's ornate, hand-drawn maps complement the entertaining commentary. *£6.95*

TEA SHOP WALKS in LANCASHIRE

Clive Price

Enjoy breathtaking upland scenery, lush river valleys or impressive coastal paths - followed by afternoon tea! A refreshing blend of walks and tea shops that helps you get the very best out of Lancashire. *£6.95*

MERSEYSIDE MEANDERS

Michael Smout

Here are 31 walks to celebrate the pleasures of walking in the Merseyside area. A few are city walks, but most are through open land, fields or coastline. Many well-known places including Liverpool, Aintree, Halewood and Southport - but such gems as Port Sunlight, Thurstaston and Ness await you with their fascinating heritage, history and ecological interest. *£7.95*

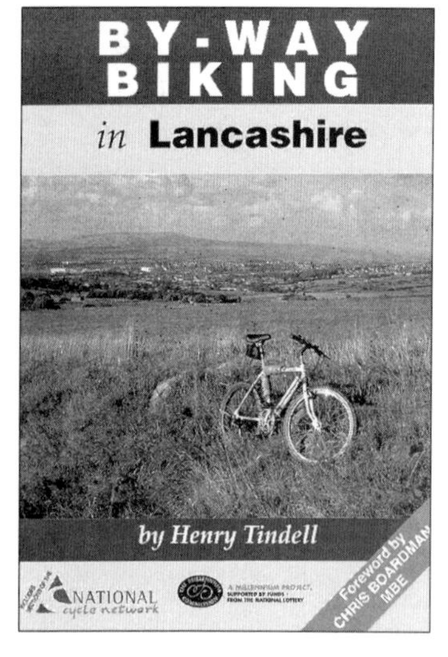

BY-WAY BIKING in LANCASHIRE

Henry Tindell

Discover Lancashire's hidden beauty and outstanding potential as a destination for mountain bikers along a fine variety of off-road tracks and country lanes. *£7.95*

All of our books are available through booksellers. In case of difficulty, or for a free catalogue, please contact:
SIGMA LEISURE, 1 SOUTH OAK LANE, WILMSLOW, CHESHIRE SK9 6AR.
Phone: 01625-531035
Fax: 01625-536800.
E-mail: info@sigmapress.co.uk
Web site: http//www.sigmapress.co.uk

MASTERCARD and VISA orders welcome.